Effective Expert Witnessing

Fourth Edition

Practices for the 21st Century

Effective Expert Witnessing

Fourth Edition

Practices for the 21st Century

Jack V. Matson

Suha F. Daou

Jeffrey G. Soper

CRC Press
Taylor & Francis Group
Boca Raton London New York

CRC Press is an imprint of the
Taylor & Francis Group, an **informa** business

CRC Press
Taylor & Francis Group
6000 Broken Sound Parkway NW, Suite 300
Boca Raton, FL 33487-2742

Reissued 2019 by CRC Press

A Library of Congress record exists under LC control number:

Publisher's Note
The publisher has gone to great lengths to ensure the quality of this reprint but points out that some imperfections in the original copies may be apparent.

Disclaimer
The publisher has made every effort to trace copyright holders and welcomes correspondence from those they have been unable to contact.

ISBN 13: 978-0-367-22929-0 (hbk)
ISBN 13: 978-0-367-22933-7 (pbk)
ISBN 13: 978-0-429-27766-5 (ebk)

Visit the Taylor & Francis Web site at http://www.taylorandfrancis.com and the CRC Press Web site at http://www.crcpress.com

Preface

The judicial system is in a state of revolution and chaos with respect to expert witnessing. The *Daubert* guidelines for expert scientific testimony promulgated by the U.S. Supreme Court in 1993 are a significant part of litigation in federal court and in most state courts. The *Kumho* decision subsequently extended the guidelines to experts in all fields. Other Supreme Court and Federal Appeals Court decisions have further defined the limits and extent of the guidelines. Various State Appeals and Supreme Court decisions have included modifications and additions to the *Daubert/Kumho* guidelines.

All these actions have essentially produced trials within trials. An expert has to anticipate that the opposing council will file a motion to exclude her opinions based on nonadherence to the guidelines and that some form of a hearing may be held (depending on the judge) to qualify or exclude the expert. The judge must decide whether the expert has the proper credentials and whether the opinions are relevant and reliable. The superior advocate may win out over the best technical argument because the judge may have no way to objectively evaluate the scientific basis for the expert opinion. Confusion also results from trying to distill the difference between the methods used by the experts and the interpretation of facts that are inputs into the methodology. Where does methodology stop and interpretation of facts begin? While many a motion to exclude challenges both the method and the factual interpretation, a thoughtful reading of *Daubert* and subsequent legal precedents should limit judicial review to only the question of methodology.

The Fourth Edition represents a major departure from the previous editions. First, the *Daubert/Kumho* guidelines are not only explained in detail but also elaborated on through numerous references to interpretations by other commentators. Second, the book is extensively referenced to bring in a variety of opinions on the processes and procedures of experts. Third, the text was constructed in a more readable way, so that the newcomers to expert witnessing can more easily grasp the important concepts. Fourth, a CD video is enclosed to visually show how an expert functions in litigation. Vital information as to how to interact with attorneys, how to handle a deposition, and how to give testimony at trial are demonstrated in mock form. Also, inside tips are provided at each important juncture. Fifth, the book was constructed to fulfill the needs of all expert witnesses irrespective of discipline or field.

Throughout this edition, I have made extensive reference to the Federal Rules of Civil Procedure and the Federal Rules of Evidence. Although some state courts have adopted rules that parallel the Federal Rules, many have not. In addition, many individual federal district and circuit courts have adopted their own "local" rules that may supplement the general rules. If you are involved in litigation as a testifying expert, consult with the attorneys for whom you work to determine what rules of procedure or evidence will govern your participation in the case.

In the prior edition, I commented that expert witnessing has become more challenging. That turned out to be an understatement. I recall an old Kit Carson quote related to those traveling by wagon train across the western U.S. in the mid-1800s, "The cowards never start, and the weak die along the way." So it is with expert witnessing. Hopefully, this book will provide an essential knowledge base for you to start confidently and maintain your strength along the way in meeting the challenges.

The Authors

Jack V. Matson, Ph.D., is Professor of Environmental Engineering at Pennsylvania State University and owner of Matson and Associates LLC, a litigation support consulting engineering firm, in State College, PA. His expertise is in the field of chemical emissions, water and wastewater treatment, air pollution, hazardous waste, and standard of care. He teaches and conducts research in those technical areas. Dr. Matson has a B.S. and an M.S. in Chemical Engineering from the University of Toledo and a Ph.D. in Environmental Engineering from Rice University. He also attended the University of Michigan Law School. His work experience includes process engineering for the Sun Oil Refinery in Toledo, OH; chemical and environmental engineering for Enjay (now Exxon) Chemicals in Baytown, TX; and management of environmental engineering projects for S&B Engineers and Contractors in Houston, TX. He was on the faculty at the University of Houston from 1974 to 1992 and is currently at Pennsylvania State University, having completed his 29th year in academia. From 1991 to 1993, he was appointed to the Texas Air Control Board as a regulator and was Chair of the Enforcement and Regulation Development Committees. Dr. Matson began as an expert witness in the mid-1970s and, over the years, has been deposed in over 100 cases and has given testimony at 15 trials. He can be reached at Box 408, State College, PA, 16804-0408; e-mail: jvm4@psu.edu; phone: 814-231-5253.

Jeff Soper, Ph.D., is a member of the faculty at the University of Tampa, where he serves as an Associate Professor of Management, Associate Director of the TECO Center for Leadership, and the Senior Research Fellow at the Human Resource Institute. He has facilitated numerous professional and management development programs in a wide range of topics ranging from leadership development, ethics, and change management to creativity, innovation, and organization development. He coauthored the *ASTD Models for Workplace Learning and Development*. Dr. Soper earned a B.S. in Technology and Management from the University of Maryland, an M.B.A. from Columbia University, and a Ph.D. in Workforce Education and Development from Pennsylvania State University, specializing in Human Resource Development.

Suha F. Daou, Ph.D., is a senior partner in *LIPP*artners, Inc., specializing in training and development. She has provided a variety of human and organizational performance improvement efforts, which encompassed comprehensive needs assessment, training materials development for various delivery media, train-the-trainer programs, selection and performance appraisal guidelines, and training evaluation programs in a wide range of project areas. Dr. Daou earned a B.A. in Psychology and an M.A. in Educational Psychology from American University of Beirut, as well as a Ph.D. in Workforce Education and Development from Pennsylvania State University.

Acknowledgments

I thank Ms. Michelle Katz for her legal expertise and dedicated assistance in editing this book. I would also like to thank Dr. Richard Schumann, Ms. Wendy Pearson, and the late Dr. Colin Baynes, for their expert collaborations over the years.

Jack V. Matson

Table of Contents

Section II

Section I

The Legal Environment and Expert Witnessing

I was never ruined but twice: once when I lost a lawsuit and once when I won one.

—**Voltaire**

1

The Legal Environment

An expert is an individual who was not present when the "incident" occurred, but for a healthy fee will happily imagine what it was like and how it happened.

—Justin P. Murphy

What is litigation? It is a legal proceeding between two or more parties in an attempt to "right" an alleged wrong. The "right" usually takes the form of a demand for payment to the party alleging injury. The path to a legal solution is often filled with unanticipated twists, unexpected delays, and potentially high stress for even the most seasoned litigants. Litigation is more often about losing less than it is about winning more; a litigant "is a person about to give up his skin in the hope of retaining his bone." (Ambrose Bierce). Understanding the basic rules and practices of litigation can help you prepare for your role as an expert witness.

Lawyers and Litigation

An anonymous author once wrote that "America is a country where, thanks to Congress, there are 40 million laws to enforce 10 Commandments." As a result, litigation can easily take long periods of time and a great deal of expense. As courts become more congested with the seemingly endless number of cases being filed, the process can bog down from sheer volume alone. To be fair, many of the cases filed have merit. The American legal system is built on the principle of protecting the rights of the individual, and litigation is one way to protect those rights. Merit or not, however, the number of lawsuits continues to grow with little sign of slowing. Lawyers are the vanguards of the justice system. The American Bar Association's Model Rules of Professional Conduct provide attorneys with a framework for carrying out their responsibilities to their clients, the courts, and society in a professional manner. These rules are particularly important when pursuing a client's claims, given the adversarial nature of litigation as well as the conflicts that may arise when lawyer and client have differing interests in the outcome (for example, settling a case versus taking it to trial).

The Model Rules require lawyers to provide "competent representation" to their clients in the areas of legal knowledge, skill, thoroughness, and preparation. Legal knowledge includes knowledge of federal and state rules of evidence and civil procedure, as well as precedents set by case law, in order "to advance and protect the integrity of the fact-finding process."[1] Mastering these laws not only helps lawyers and their clients but also reduces the possibility for embarrassment and legal complications such as mistrials, inadmissible evidence, lost appeals, or reversed verdicts.[2]

The litigation process begins with a conversation between a potential client and the attorney who may represent him or her. In these initial discussions, the client provides the attorney with details about the incident that caused injury, damage, or loss.[3] After collecting facts, perceptions, and opinions from the potential client, the attorney analyzes this information and collects additional data to determine if the potential client has a viable case. Next, the attorney assesses the financial, legal, and philosophical viability of the case by reviewing applicable questions of law, statutes, circumstances, precedents, and potential damage judgments.[4] Based upon this assessment, the lawyer determines whether to accept or reject the case. If the lawyer decides to accept the case, the attorney-client relationship is formed; the

[1] Michael E. Sacks, *An overview of the law: A guide for testifying and consulting experts* (Horsham, PA: LRP Publications, 1995), 2.

[2] Sacks.

[3] Marc A. Rabinoff and Stephen P. Holmes, *The forensic expert's guide to litigation: The anatomy of a lawsuit* (Horsham, PA: LRP Publications, 1996), 1.

[4] Rabinoff and Holmes, 2.

relation is documented in an agreement that clarifies the responsibilities and expectations of each party.

When all of these steps have been achieved, the attorney files a complaint in court, articulating the client's grievances and enumerating the relief that the client — now the plaintiff — seeks from the court. Thus begins litigation: a complicated, thorough, and at times arduous process, but extremely important for resolving disputes. Unfortunately, initiating litigation, even in the most meritorious of cases, does not guarantee a positive outcome. Nonetheless, parties and their lawyers pursue litigation — both as plaintiffs and as defendants — for reasons ranging from the pursuit of justice to the desire for money (or in the case of defendants, the desire to avoid paying). Attorneys accept the uncertainty of outcome, even when they are paid on a contingency basis, because that is the way litigation works. If the attorney is skilled in both litigation and the selection of cases, "the profit is in the volume and the key is to keep on plugging."[5] The outcome of any case ultimately can depend on the presentation of evidence before a judge or jury who will sort out the merits of the claims and defenses and render a judgment. For the plaintiff, the desire for a favorable judgment and an award of damages — in essence, the desire to win — is what keeps the parties and lawyers motivated.

Evidence

The probability of winning increases with the skillful presentation of evidence. Evidence is information presented to a court to support or refute a case or a position in a lawsuit. Evidence may include oral testimony as well as tangible material such as documents, exhibits, and demonstrative aids. Evidence is critical to the outcome of a case, since juries decide verdicts based upon the evidence. However, not all evidence in a case is heard by the jury; only evidence that is relevant and admissible plays a role in the outcome of a case.

The admission of evidence in federal court is governed by the Federal Rules of Evidence. These rules were adopted in 1975 to provide a uniform guideline that specifically addresses the admissibility of evidence. Rule 104 establishes that the judge decides whether an individual is competent to be a witness and whether particular evidence is admissible. Rule 104(b) gives the scope of the judge's responsibility. It states that "the judge may admit evidence — which otherwise might be ruled irrelevant — contingent upon the fulfillment of a condition of fact or subject to the introduction of other evidence which establishes a fact."

[5] Peter W. Huber, *Galileo's revenge: Junk science in the courtroom* (New York: Basic Books, 1991), 70.

Rule 401 of the Federal Rules of Evidence addresses what kind of evidence is relevant. Evidence is relevant if it has "any tendency to make the existence of any fact that is of consequence to the determination of the action more probable or less probable than it would be without the evidence." Relevant evidence must be pertinent to the issue in the case and is admitted only if it will help the jury make a decision. The burden of proof of relevancy rests on the proponent of the evidence (the party that will benefit from the introduction and admission of the evidence). The opposing attorney may object to the proffered (potential) evidence on the grounds that it is inadmissible or irrelevant. After hearing the positions offered by each attorney, the judge decides whether to admit the evidence. That decision is not based on the veracity or persuasiveness of the evidence, but only on the narrow question of whether the jury should be permitted to hear the testimony.

Evidence with moderate, marginal, or questionable relevancy will not be admitted. Additionally, though evidence may be relevant, it still may not be admitted, based on Federal Rule of Evidence 403. Rule 403 excludes evidence, even though relevant, on the grounds of prejudice, confusion, misleading the jury, unfounded delay, or waste of time.

Likewise, there are circumstances under which irrelevant evidence may still be admitted. Rule 104 empowers the judge to admit evidence that seems irrelevant or inappropriate but that may prove to be relevant later in the proceedings, in light of other evidence that has been admitted. For example, evidence that is hypothetical or based on conjecture, as opposed to evidence that describes something that actually happened, may still be admitted under Rule 104 if that evidence is based on the facts of the case and would be helpful to the jury in resolving the case.

Such evidence is most often introduced through the testimony of expert witnesses. An expert is a person who, by reason of education or special training, possesses knowledge of a particular subject area in greater depth than does the public at large. Rule 702 allows the admission of expert testimony only if the testimony will be helpful to the judge or jury in deciding the facts, and if the expert possesses appropriate qualifications to testify on the subject in which he or she purports to be an expert. To do this, the judge must analyze whether the expert's testimony is (1) sufficiently based on reliable facts or data (and not merely on hypothetical circumstances), (2) the product of reliable principles and methods, and (3) the result of a reliable application of those principles and methods to the facts. Since Rule 104 vests the judge with the sole authority to determine the admissibility of evidence, it is the responsibility of the judge to determine whether to accept or reject the testimony of an expert witness, based on Rule 702.

The Role of the Expert Witness

With the increasing complexity of cases, particularly those that require the resolution of scientific or technical questions, the expert witness has become critical to the success of litigation. The language of Rule 702 suggests that experts have a significant advantage over ordinary witnesses because they are "the only witnesses who are permitted to reflect, opine, and pontificate. Experts can provide a bridge between the particular facts of a case and patterns of fact that can be observed and understood only through much wider study."[6]

Experts generally are viewed as positive contributors in litigation. However, experts also can be portrayed as "liars" and "hired guns." Either way, one thing is certain — the use of experts is pervasive. In fact, experts have become synonymous with trials. According to Robert R. Detlefsen, "The expert witness has become a fixture in high-stakes civil trials."[7] This is true for a wide variety of reasons, not the least of which are the increasing complexity of subjects that constitute modern tort litigation and the ever-changing proceedings in the regulation of business practices.[8] "The use of experts in courtroom trials is so prevalent today that the question confronting litigators is usually not whether to hire an expert witness, but rather how many to employ and where to find them."[9]

What Is an Expert Witness?

The Rules of Evidence recognize two categories of witnesses. Lay witnesses, also called percipient or fact witnesses, are called to testify because they have seen, heard, or done something relevant to the facts and circumstances of the case. The testimony of such witnesses contributes directly to establishing the factual events.

As noted earlier, an expert witness is a person who, by reasons of education or special training, possesses knowledge of a particular subject that may be beyond the understanding of the average person. Experts are not always required. They are hired only if their expertise is necessary to present technical and/or complex facts, or to provide expert opinions based upon their knowledge, experience, and qualifications.

The contribution of expert witnesses is not limited to their personal knowledge. Expert witnesses can draw inferences from ordinary science, business, or other technical areas. They may be asked to offer opinions on

[6] Huber, 204.
[7] Robert R. Detlefsen, Confronting hostile experts in the court of public opinion, *The Metropolitan Corporate Counsel* (May 2001), 20.
[8] Detlefsen, 20.
[9] Detlefsen, 20.

the cause or consequence of occurrences. They may even be called upon to interpret the actions of others and the impact of those actions on liability. The opinions and observations of expert witnesses increase the probability of reaching a fair and just ruling because expert witnesses are able to explain facts that might otherwise escape notice and consideration. As a result, expert witnesses are most often challenged on the reliability of their interpretations of the facts and on the objectivity or bias of their testimony.

How Expert Witnesses Are Used

Just as the nature of an expert witness's testimony varies, so does the role of the expert witness. In some cases, the expert witness is used to identify problems or defects in the testimony of fact witnesses. In other cases, expert testimony is necessary to meet the burden of proof in order to establish a claim or defense. At times, expert witnesses are used primarily to match the opponent's experts and to add persuasive strength to the proponent's claim or defense.

Although experts are most commonly identified with their role as testifying witnesses in deposition or at trials, they also can assist attorneys in the development of the case before trial. Lawyers may hire experts to evaluate the credentials and work of other experts. Experts also may assist lawyers in understanding the technical aspects of a case by reviewing records and documents produced by the parties and by identifying and evaluating issues in a case. In addition, experts can help formulate requests for documents and other information which may become admissible evidence, or they can prepare questions for direct and cross-examination of witnesses. Expert advice may be critical in avoiding a case being dismissed by the court before trial by establishing persuasive theories of causation which should be heard and evaluated by the jury.

Another important function of expert witnesses may be to conduct tests or experiments related to an element involved in the litigation and to prepare demonstrative evidence illustrating their conclusions and the basis for them. To do so, tests and experiments must be painstakingly and extensively planned, documented, and recorded. Experts must be able to defend each step of the testing and experimental process to explain how laboratory conditions relate to the actual facts and circumstances of the case.

Types of Experts

There are two types of experts: consulting and testifying. The distinction between the two is critical because it has an impact on the disclosure of information, thoughts, and processes. Consulting experts provide background knowledge and lend their expertise outside of the courtroom. A consulting expert is used as a resource in complicated and technical areas in which lawyers have little background, often instructing and guiding lawyers on unfamiliar subject matter. A consulting expert will not be called as a witness. Testifying experts, on the other hand, go beyond the support provided by consulting experts and ultimately assist the lawyers trying a case by providing testimony either in court or in depositions.

The distinction between a testifying expert and a consulting expert is important because the identity and opinions of testifying experts must be revealed to the opposing party in advance of trial if properly requested. This means the opposing side will have access to the experts and their records and, therefore, be better able to prepare a response. Rule 26(4)(a) of the Federal Rules of Civil Procedure provides that the discovery of the facts known and opinions held by experts, otherwise discoverable and acquired or developed in anticipation of litigation or for trial, may be obtained only through interrogatories requiring the party to identify the expert he expects to call as a witness at trial, the subject matter on which the expert is expected to testify, the substance of the facts and opinions to which the expert is expected to testify, and a summary of the grounds for each opinion.[10] Additionally, testifying experts are required to reveal all materials provided to them by attorneys and to provide data and pertinent information used to form opinions. This data and information includes but is not limited to papers, articles, memos, calculations, and facts used to prepare the expert's report.

The rules governing consulting experts differ from those that govern testifying experts and are determined by the type of consulting expert involved. Consulting experts can be divided into three categories. The first consists of experts who do not testify but who are hired either in preparation for trial or in anticipation of litigation. The opinions of these experts can be discovered only in exceptional circumstances. The discovery of their opinions and the data upon which the opinions are based are subject to and limited by Rule 26(4)(b). The second category consists of experts who are consulted informally in preparation for trial. The identities and/or opinions of individuals within this category of consulting experts need not be revealed and cannot be discovered. The third category includes experts who have personal knowledge about the facts that led to the suit or experts working for a particular party but whose knowledge and information were not acquired to prepare for trial. This category includes employees of a party not specifically employed in support of the suit and experts who participated in or viewed the occurrences that gave rise to the suit. These experts are not included within Federal Rules of Civil Procedure Rule (26)(4)(b); "therefore all facts and opinions they have are freely discoverable as with any ordinary witness."[11]

[10] Robert C. Clifford, *Qualifying and attacking expert witnesses* (Santa Ana, CA: James Publishing Group, 1990).

[11] Clifford, 102.

Because the identity of the consulting expert is not discoverable in most states, consulting experts can assist a lawyer in ways that testifying experts cannot. All communication between attorneys and consulting experts is protected from discovery. This protection encourages free and open discussion between attorneys and consulting experts. Attorneys often use consulting experts for brainstorming prior to and in preparation for trial. Mental impressions, opinions, and the identity of the consulting expert need be revealed only "if they form the bases of opinion of an expert who will testify at trial."[12]

Because of the distinct differences in rules between the two types of experts, the work of consulting experts and that of testifying experts should be kept separate. Successful lawyers strategically balance the use of testifying and consulting experts in order to protect their cases.

The Relationship between Lawyers and Experts

Lawyers expect experts to be confident, persuasive, and impartial, yet not boastful or contentious. They want experts who are firm, with strength of conviction. They need experts who will explain technical, complex matters in a way that the jury fully understands and to which jurors can relate. Lawyers also want experts with appropriate credentials to support narrowly tailored opinions that will serve the lawyers' objectives at trial. While communication and teaching skills may be more important than credentials for a testifying expert, outstanding expertise and analytical ability may be more important than the ability to communicate and teach for a nontestifying, or consulting, expert. Thus, the lawyer's expectations will change depending on how the expert will be used.

In turn, experts expect lawyers to provide a complete and thorough explanation of the case, the key issues and challenges, and the fundamental standards of proof from a legal perspective. They expect to be provided with all relevant information and documentation to which the lawyer is privy as soon as physically possible.

Lawyers should respect the ethics and professional integrity of the expert and not demand that opinions be slanted in order to bolster the case. Experts need lawyers to clearly describe and explain the interrelationships between their testimonies and those of other experts involved in the case so the experts can prepare to explain conflicts of opinion.

Experts also expect attorneys to educate them about the nature of the legal proceedings and vocabulary, as well as what is expected of the expert

[12] Ernest Reynolds III, The selection and use of the defense expert, (State Bar of Texas Professional Development Program, Experts in litigation: A performance enhancement course 1987) C23; and Knox D. Nunnally, Use of experts, (State Bar of Texas Professional Development Advanced Personal Injury Law Course, 1987) U16.

at each juncture. In a positive working relationship with a lawyer, an expert will be treated as a peer over the course of the case and will be actively involved in developing case strategy, based on the objective, impartial, and independent findings of the expert.

The Expert Report

An expert witness may need to submit an expert report prior to trial. The requirements for an expert report differ according to whether a case is pending in federal or state court. Federal rules require expert witnesses to prepare reports and provide them to the opposing parties, although this requirement can be waived if directed by the court or agreed to by the principal parties involved. Some state courts do not require expert reports but may request other forms of obligatory disclosure. Regardless of the requirement, the expert report is an important document that lawyer and expert alike must understand.

An expert report must be prepared and signed by the expert who developed it. The expert report should express the opinions of the expert and provide the basis, rationale, data, or information used to reach, and exhibits to support, the opinions provided. The report should address explicitly the factors for reliability and relevance. In federal court, the report must also provide the expert's qualifications, any relevant publications developed within the last ten years, any compensation received for conduct of the study and testimony provided in the case, and a list of cases in which the expert was involved within the previous four years. The expert report is discussed in greater detail in Chapter 4.

Regardless of how the expert is used or the method through which expertise and opinions are communicated, the key objective of the expert witness is to clearly and persuasively present his or her understanding of the facts and issues to the jury in the form of an opinion. Opposite conclusions may be drawn from the same set of facts, depending on how the facts are interpreted. The success of the case can hinge on the effectiveness of expert witnesses and, ultimately, on their presentation and testimony in deposition or at trial.

2

Key Cases and Precedents Affecting Expert Witnessing

One expert to another: "What did your attorney tell you?" "He told me to tell the truth." "Did he say anything else?" "Yes, he told me what the truth was."

—Anonymous

Though expert witnesses have been used for centuries in Europe, they were rare in the United States until the 1920s. The Supreme Court had been cautious in using experts and limited their cross-examination, which was perceived as a waste of time, exhausting and confusing to the court and jury instead of clarifying the issues at hand.[1] Then, in 1923, the United States Circuit Court of Appeals for the District of Columbia Circuit issued a landmark decision that defined the basic prerequisite for admitting scientific evidence and, thus, testimony by expert witnesses.

[1] Marcia Angell, *Science on trial: The clash of medical evidence and the law in the breast implant case*, 1st ed. (New York: W.W. Norton & Company, 1996).

Frye v. United States (1923)

Frye v. United States[2] delineated the threshold requirement for the admissibility of scientific evidence; this requirement became the standard recognized by most courts for the next seventy years. In *Frye*, the defendant was accused of second-degree murder. The defense attorney offered the testimony of an expert witness to administer and interpret the results of a polygraph test. At that time, the polygraph test was conducted by measuring changes in the blood pressure of the subject as he or she answered a variety of questions. If the subject responded truthfully, there would be negligible change in blood pressure; if not, the polygraph would record a spike or dramatic change. The *Frye* defendant sought the admission of polygraph results to prove that he had not committed the crime.

On appeal, the Circuit Court held that expert testimony is admissible only if founded on methods, principles, and procedures agreed upon as valid by the scientific community. The court refused to admit the expert's testimony or the polygraph test, stating that, "while courts will go a long way in admitting expert testimony deduced from a well-recognized scientific principle or discovery, the methodology from which the deduction is made must be sufficiently established to have gained general acceptance in the particular field in which it belongs."[3] Although the *Frye* defendant lost his bid to admit polygraph results, the "general acceptance" test articulated in the case opened the door for the use of scientific evidence and expert witnesses throughout the U.S. court system.

The Frye Test requires the trial court to consider two factors before admitting expert testimony. First, the court must identify the witness's expertise in a specific field of science. An individual can be considered an expert if he or she possesses the requisite education, experience, and recognizable contribution to the field, as demonstrated through activities such as the publication of peer-reviewed articles. If the witness qualifies as an expert, the second step is for the court to determine whether methods, theories, and conclusions of the expert meet the "general acceptance" standard.

The Frye Test emphasized the consensus of the scientific community in determining the validity of scientific method. Consensus is reached when scientists evaluate the quality of a proposed scientific theory through peer review, publication, criticism, replication, and determination of reliability in predicting future results.[4] In expressly limiting the admission of scientific evidence to that accepted in the general scientific community, the *Frye* court

[2] *Frye v. United States*, 293 F. 1013 (D.C. Cir. 1923).
[3] 293 F. at 1014
[4] Angell.

left no room for new, emerging, or novel scientific theories that might support a party's claim.

While the Frye Test helped define both who is an expert and what expert testimony is admissible, it was not without its problems. Key among these problems was that science is always changing; what is "generally accepted" in the scientific community is always subject to change as new theories and principles emerge. However, under most interpretations of the *Frye* standard, novel scientific theories and techniques could be deemed inadmissible, even when the expert offering the testimony possessed excellent credentials, simply because that theory was not generally accepted by the relevant scientific community.

When the Federal Rules of Evidence were adopted in 1975, the Rules Committee declined to incorporate the Frye Test in the rule governing the admissibility of expert testimony. Instead, the Rules allow the admission of testimony by experts "if scientific, technical, or other specialized knowledge will assist the trier of fact to understand the evidence or to determine a fact."[5] Nonetheless, approximately half of all states continued to apply the Frye Test to determine whether to admit the testimony of an expert witness in a scientific or technical field. Proponents contended that the "general acceptance" standard established by *Frye* ensured reliability of evidence based on established science, promoted uniformity of decisions, and expedited the trial process by reducing arguments concerning the admissibility and reliability of testimony.[6] Through the application of the Frye Test, judges, most of whom are not scientifically trained, did not have to look very closely at the scientific methodologies proffered by an expert and could defer to the scientific community on questions of general acceptance.

Daubert v. Merrell Dow Pharmaceuticals, Inc. (1993)

Even though the Frye Test was ostensibly rejected when the Rules of Evidence were adopted, it was another eighteen years before the United States Supreme Court squarely addressed what standard governed the admission of scientific and technical evidence in federal court. In the interim, federal courts were left to exercise their discretion. Rules 701 and 702 provided only the broadest of parameters for the admission of scientific evidence, with no further guidance in the Committee Notes to the Rules. Some courts, faced with ambiguities of the Rules, continued to rely on *Frye*.

One example is the class action lawsuit filed on behalf of 15,000 Vietnam War veterans who had been exposed to the chemical defoliant Agent Orange.

[5] Fed. R. Civ. P. 702

[6] *The Matrimonial Strategist*.

A relationship between Agent Orange and the medical symptoms and maladies experienced by Vietnam veterans was shown in toxicological studies conducted on animals. However, epidemiological studies did not indicate causation by Agent Orange. The judge, after screening and evaluating the scientific evidence presented by experts prior to the trial, ruled that the results of the animal and toxicological studies were inadmissible as evidence because the science did not meet the minimum standards of reliability.

In a vast departure from the prevailing Frye Test, the judge made an independent assessment of the reliability of the proffered scientific evidence, rather than relying solely on whether the methodologies used and conclusions drawn by the experts were "generally accepted" in the scientific community. This case foreshadowed reforms in the law concerning scientific evidence and expert testimony, triggered primarily by two factors: the restrictiveness of the Frye Test and the need to ensure that scientific evidence admitted in court was reliable and relevant, even if not "generally accepted."

In 1993, the United States Supreme Court decided *Daubert v. Merrill Dow Pharmaceuticals*,[7] one of the most influential cases to set the standard for the admission of scientific evidence in light of the Federal Rules of Evidence. In *Daubert*, the plaintiffs claimed that their infants' birth defects were the result of the mothers ingesting Bendectin, a drug manufactured by Merrill Dow, to combat the symptoms of morning sickness. At the time, Bendectin was very popular and was prescribed for pregnant women almost as commonly as vitamins. From 1958 to 1983, more than 17 million women took Bendectin[8], considered by the drug manufacturer to be a relatively safe and effective drug. At the time of the suit, more than thirty published studies indicated that Bendectin did not cause birth defects in unborn babies.

However, the plaintiffs' attorneys presented the testimony of eight experts who claimed that Bendectin did cause birth defects. The testimony of these eight experts was based upon science that included reworked epidemiological statistics, plus animal and toxicological studies, showing that the chemical structures of the drug were similar to those of other chemicals known to cause birth defects. The defense argued that the reanalysis of statistical data had not been published or subjected to peer review and, therefore, was not generally accepted by the scientific community. The court rejected the toxicological evidence and dismissed the plaintiffs' case on summary judgment. On appeal, the court affirmed the decision, finding that the unpublished statistical reanalysis of previously published studies was problematic because the reliability of a scientific technique does not vary according to the circumstances of each case.

[7] *Daubert v. Merrell Dow Pharmaceuticals, Inc.*, 509 U.S. 579 (1993).

[8] Angell.

The Supreme Court then heard the case and, for the first time, rejected *Frye* as the sole standard for the admissibility of scientific evidence. Noting the passage of the Federal Rules of Evidence, the Court held it was within the purview of trial judges to exercise their discretion in admitting expert testimony; trial courts were, in effect, "gatekeepers" for such admissions. The Court further held that the gatekeeping function required a case-by-case evaluation of the admissibility of an expert's testimony. The Court identified four factors courts should use to determine the reliability of scientific expert opinions:

1. The science can and has been tested.
2. The science has been subjected to peer review and publication.
3. The known or potential error rate of the science.
4. The general acceptance of the science in the relevant scientific community.

While these factors were intended to be non-exhaustive, federal courts have by and large applied them to the admission of expert testimony without regard to other factors. These criteria have become the " *Daubert* Test." Over the years, the body of law developed since *Daubert* has elucidated the meaning of the factors.

1. *The science can and has been tested.* This factor has been interpreted to mean that the theory upon which the science relies has been verified through the scientific method in the laboratory, in the field, or both. Data must have been collected, analyzed, and related back to scientific theory. Others must have tested the theory and found under what conditions it was valid. Any algorithm or model based on scientific theory can be used as long as it meets these conditions.
2. *The science has been subjected to peer review and publication.* The reliability of the science must be proven through literature published in peer-reviewed journals. Peer review is generally defined as a process by which the manuscript is sent to reviewers in the relevant field. To be published, the manuscript must satisfy the reviewers. The decision to publish a paper is typically based on the soundness of the science and its impact in the field. Professional textbooks, government publications, and articles in journals fall in this category. Peer-reviewed abstracts and papers given at conferences (and published in the proceedings) fall in a gray area. Studies and reports not sent out for external scrutiny and publication are not considered peer-reviewed.
3. *The known or potential error rate of the science.* "Error rate" is the expected error associated with a scientific method or technique, based

upon available data, applied data, and the testing environment. It can be described in various ways, such as error percentages, statistical confidence levels, units of plausibility, boundary conditions, etc. Just because a technique may have a high error rate does not mean it is unreliable. Error rates, to some degree, represent the state of knowledge in a particular area on available data. Thus, error rates must be examined in context of the scientific area applied and the degree of certainty or correlation necessary to form a reliable expert opinion.

4. *The general acceptance of the science in the relevant scientific community.* This factor echoes the standard for admission that prevailed for so long under *Frye.* It is attributed to the weight members of the relevant scientific community give the evidence, based on their consensus of what is acceptable science and under what conditions. Novel science in any field is always being developed, while old science is always in the process of being challenged, modified, and made obsolete. The general acceptance factor can be a severe limitation in the courtroom because the new science may in fact be better, more reliable, and more relevant than the old science. Under *Daubert*, general acceptance is not definitive; it is expected to be applied by the courts as one of many factors. The judge has the discretion to allow new science as long as it can be shown that it is demonstratively better and meets other criteria, such as peer review.

The practical effect of these changes is that experts are likely to be subjected to a *Daubert* challenge to exclude the expert's testimony prior to the trial. The judge's decisions on a *Daubert* motion can decide the fate of the case if that expert is essential to proving the cause of action. Thus, it is imperative that experts understand the factors for admissibility of science-based expert opinions."Whether the specific *Daubert* factors are appropriate measures of reliability in a particular case is a matter the law grants the trial judge broad latitude to determine — the same broad latitude that the trial judge enjoys with respect to his or her ultimate reliability determination."[9] Many trial courts have turned *Daubert* into a rigid test, using the four factors as if they were carved in stone. In those courts, an expert has to satisfy each and every one of the factors in order to qualify as a witness.[10] The need for a set of standards or guidelines that addressed the limitations of the Frye Test was a primary reason the Supreme Court heard *Daubert*, yet in its application, it has accorded no more flexibility than *Frye*, and in many cases has become

[9] Robert F. Reilly, Accountants' considerations of *Daubert*-related decisions on valuation expert testimony, *The National Public Accountant* (October 2000), 13.
[10] Branch, T.W. From the "Frye"-ing pan into the tire. (Albuquerque, NM: Branch Law Firm.)

more restrictive. Also, it has led in many instances to pretrial hearings where the expert has to defend his or her opinions.

Shortly after *Daubert*, the Supreme Court decided two other cases that significantly shaped the way courts evaluate the admissibility of expert evidence. Together with *Daubert*, these cases are often described as the "*Daubert* Trilogy." Few trial courts decide *Daubert* motions without reference to *General Electric v. Joiner*, which established the standard of review for *Daubert* decisions, and *Carmichael v. Kumho Tire Company*, which expanded the scope of *Daubert* to all experts, not only experts on scientific matters.

General Electric v. Joiner (1997)

In *General Electric v. Joiner*,[11] Joiner, an electrician working for General Electric, claimed that he developed lung cancer as a result of being exposed to polychlorinated biphenyls (PCBs), a toxic chemical. The judge held that the scientific testimony in support of this claim was not admissible because it failed to show the relationship between PCBs and lung cancer, in what the court referred to as an "analytical gap." Accordingly, the plaintiff's case was dismissed on summary judgment. On appeal, the Circuit Court reversed the decision. In reaching its decision, the Court reasoned that because the Federal Rules of Evidence favor the admissibility of evidence, a decision to exclude testimony should be reviewed on a stricter standard than that governing a decision to admit testimony.

The Supreme Court reversed, holding that "abuse of discretion" is the correct standard for reviewing a trial court's decision to admit or exclude an expert's testimony. However, unlike in *Daubert*, where the Court remanded the case to the trial court, the Supreme Court itself examined the record and found that the trial court had not abused its discretion by excluding the expert's testimony.

Moreover, in upholding the trial court's decision, the Court examined not only the scientific methodology employed by the expert, but also the conclusions drawn by the expert to establish causation. The plaintiffs had argued that an examination of the conclusions violated the precept in *Daubert* that the trial court's "focus, of course, must be solely on the principles and methodology, not on the conclusions they generate." Nonetheless, in *Joiner*, the Court stated that where the expert's conclusions and the basis for those conclusions do not flow rationally from the purported methodology, the expert's testimony may be properly excluded. The Rules of Evidence and *Daubert*, the *Joiner* court held, do not require the admission of testimony solely because the expert says the conclusion follows the methodology.

[11] *General Electric Co., et al. v. Joiner, et al.*, 522 U.S. 136 (1997).

Rather, experts are obligated to lay out carefully how the methodology and principles logically lead to their conclusions by, for example, providing a detailed expert report. This obligation, and the ability of the expert to meet it, helps parties on both sides of litigation identify experts who can rationally support, explain, and defend their conclusions.[12]

Carmichael v. Kumho Tire Company (1998)

One year after *Joiner*, the Supreme Court decided *Carmichael v. Kumho Tire Company.*[13] In *Kumho*, the Ford minivan driven by the plaintiff blew a rear tire on Interstate 65 in Baldwin County, Alabama. As a result of the blowout, the minivan overturned, killing one passenger and injuring seven. The plaintiff was the sixth owner of the Ford minivan, which had been driven more than 96,000 miles.

The survivors and the decedent's representative filed a lawsuit against the tire maker and its distributor, Kumho Tire Company, alleging that the accident was the result of a manufacturing and/or design defect. In support of this contention, Dennis Carlson, Jr., a tire failure analyst, was hired by the plaintiff to provide expert testimony confirming that a manufacturing or design defect had caused the rear tire blowout and ensuing accident. This opinion was based on two key factors: (1) a visual and tactile inspection of the tire's manufacture, and (2) "the theory that in the absence of at least two of four specific, physical symptoms indicating tire abuse, the tire failure of the sort that occurred here was caused by a defect."

The defendant, Kumho Tire Company, requested that Carlson's testimony be excluded, arguing that his testimony did not meet the Federal Rule of Evidence 702 requirement that a qualified expert witness can testify in the form of an opinion of scientific, technical, or other specialized knowledge only if the testimony will assist the trier of fact. Additionally, the defense contended that the four *Daubert* factors — testing, peer review, error rates, and acceptability in the relevant scientific community — were not identified in testimony; therefore, those factors were not met, and the Court accepted the defense contentions. Finally, the Court made it clear that the trial judge's general function of assuring that expert testimony is both reliable and relevant applies to all experts under Rule 702, not merely experts with scientific knowledge.

The *Kumho* case was significant because it clarified three key challenges facing judges in ruling on the admissibility of expert testimony under

[12] Anthony Z. Roisman, Attorney assesses what *G.E. v. Joiner* means for testifying experts, *The Testifying Expert* (March 1998), 3–4.
[13] *Kumho Tire Co. v. Carmichael,* 119 S. Ct. 1167 (1999).

Daubert. First, the Court reiterated that it is the responsibility of the jury — not the judge — to assess and evaluate different and conflicting expert testimony, even in areas where the basis of the evidence may be in question. According to the Court, "where experts might reasonably differ, [t]he jury must decide among the conflicting views of differing experts, even though the evidence is 'shaky.'"[14] The judge as gatekeeper is charged with making certain that an expert witness "employs in the courtroom the same level of intellectual rigor that characterizes the practice of an expert in the relevant field"[15] and that "vigorous cross-examination, presentation of contrary evidence, and careful instruction on the burden of proof are the traditional and appropriate means of attacking shaky but admissible evidence."[16]

Second, the *Kumho* case clearly established that the four *Daubert* factors do not constitute a definitive checklist for evaluating the reliability and relevance of expert testimony, but rather serve as a guide in such determinations. The court stated that the trial judge decides "whether the factors may or may not be pertinent in assessing reliability, depending on the nature of the issue, the expert's particular expertise, and the subject of his testimony."[17]

The third point addressed in *Kumho* concerns potential abuse of *Daubert* by defendants demanding full-blown hearings for determining the reliability and relevance of expert testimony, often without showing good cause to doubt the reliability of the expert.[18] Such actions can unduly delay trial proceedings, imposing considerable expense on plaintiffs. In *Kumho*, the Court stated that trial judges must make a reliability determination "when the basis of an expert's opinion is 'called sufficiently into question.' The Court did not go into detail, but the comment suggests that the opposing party needs to come forward with some evidence of unreliability — expert testimony or scientific literature, for example — beyond a bare objection by counsel."[19]

From the perspective of the judicial system, the Court's opinion in *Kumho,* as in *Daubert* and *Joiner*, emphasized that appellate courts must allow for flexibility on the part of trial judges, and that the appeal process should examine whether the trial court abused its discretion when deciding to admit or exclude expert testimony in "ordinary cases where the reliability of an expert's methods is properly taken for granted," rather than reassessing the evidence anew. Moreover, the Court clearly intended that the judge's gatekeeping function should not result in making litigation unduly burdensome.

[14] Mark S. Mandell, *Kumho*: Some clarity — but but not the last word — on experts, *The Testifying Expert* (June 1999), 3.
[15] Mandell, 3.
[16] Mandell, 3.
[17] Mandell, 3.
[18] Mandell, 4.
[19] Mandell, 4.

Finally, from the perspective of trial lawyers, *Kumho* helped clarify the preparation necessary to meet the threshold requirement for determining the reliability of an expert witness but did not provide a "bright line" for admissibility. Because *Kumho* held that *Daubert* clearly applies to any expert, not just scientists, increased importance was placed on making sure that every expert and each of the methodologies he employed are screened. Although an expert does not have to qualify solely on the four factors of *Daubert*, it is virtually certain that the *Daubert* criteria will be applied to his or her opinions. "Limiting testimony to experts who can prove that their theories have scientific grounding will substantially help eliminate some types of 'buccaneering" litigation.'[20]

> *Kumho* does not appear to alter any doctrines radically with respect to the admission of expert testimony. To the contrary, it explains the *Daubert* standard for admission of expert testimony and clarifies that (i) the *Daubert* test should not be limited to scientific testimony, but also testimony based upon technical and/or other specialized knowledge; (ii) the factors outlined in *Daubert* are to be applied in a flexible, rather than a rigid manner, and (iii) the decisions of the trial judge with respect to admission of expert testimony shall be reviewed under the abuse of discretion, rather than the *de novo* standard.[21]

A Note on the Hearsay Rule

Rule 801 (c) of the Federal Rules of Evidence defines hearsay as a statement, other than one made by the declarant while testifying at the trial or hearing, offered in evidence to prove the truth of the matter asserted. Rule 802 provides that hearsay is generally inadmissible. However, Rule 803 enumerates twenty-four exceptions that would allow hearsay evidence to be admitted. Rule 803 (18) of the Federal Rules of Evidence provides that "to the extent called to the attention of the expert witness on cross-examination or relied upon by the expert witness in direct examination, statements contained in published treatises, periodicals, or pamphlets on a subject of history, medicine, or other science or art are not excluded by the hearsay rule if established as a reliable authority by the testimony or admission of the witness or by

[20] Steven Brostoff, Insurers praise U.S. Supreme Court for giving judges power on 'expert' testimony, *National Underwriter* (March 29, 1999), 2.

[21] David M. Scott, Scientific v. nonscientific expert testimony: The admissibility distinction that never was, *Commercial Law Bulletin* (May-June 1999), 22.

other expert testimony or by judicial notice. If admitted, the statements may be read into evidence but may not be received as exhibits."[22]

Rule 804 addresses hearsay exceptions applicable only when the declarant is unavailable. This rule covers unavailability due to (1) exemption to testify for a reason deemed valid, (2) refusal to testify, (3) inability to remember specifics required for testifying; (4) death or illness in the family, (5) inability to locate the desired witness, or (6) failure to compel the individual to testify. Former testimony, statements made under belief of impending death, and statements against interest are also admissible as exceptions to the hearsay rule.

If an expert is withdrawn prior to trial, the prior deposition testimony of that witness is most often inadmissible as hearsay evidence. A party must be able to withdraw experts from participating in a case without fear that an abandoned expert's deposition testimony will be admitted into evidence at trial as an "admission."

The significant precedents that affect expert witnessing — including *Frye*, *Daubert*, *Joiner*, and *Kumho* — have shaped the use and solidified the value of expert testimony in the American judicial system. Understanding these precedents and the rules of hearsay are fundamental in becoming an effective expert witness. Of course, as in almost every aspect of the American judicial system, laws and precedents are subject to interpretation and varying degrees of application, as demonstrated through a closer look at the impact of *Daubert*.

[22] Fed. R. Evid. P. 803(18); Robert C. Clifford, *Qualifying and attacking expert witnesses* (Santa Ana, CA: James Publishing Group, 1990), 345.

3

A Closer Look at the Impact of *Daubert*

An expert is one who knows more and more about less and less.

—Nicholas Murray Butler

Conformity versus Flexibility

Under the landmark *Frye* decision, courts were constrained to admit scientific evidence only as long as it is was generally accepted by the scientific community. Under *Frye*, experts were expected to explain why and how their work met the test of general acceptance. The difficulty arose when the opinion of the expert departed from those generally accepted by the scientific community, regardless of merit. Under *Frye*, novel theories could not be presented to the jury, even when the expert's credentials and methodology were valid. As a result, experts could not base their testimony on new and innovative approaches until those approaches were adopted or recognized by a larger scientific community. Under this limitation, a community of experts essentially became a form of technical jury that ruled on the validity of the science before it was presented to the jury. At best, this sort of evaluation excluded junk testimony and avoided misleading the judge and the jury. However, it also limited the use of scientific evidence that had not yet gained general acceptance in the scientific community. In many circumstances, good new science takes years to become generally accepted. Thus, under *Frye*, emerging sound science that might have been of greater assistance to a jury was not available.

Under *Daubert*, federal courts were given far greater flexibility in determining the admissibility of expert scientific testimony. Rather than looking to the scientific community to determine whether scientific evidence was sufficiently sound to be considered by the trier of fact, a judge is expected to screen scientific evidence to determine its relevance and reliability. While the court is free to consider whether the methodologies used by the expert have been generally accepted, the court is also expected to inquire into the substance of those methodologies. In part, this change evolved as an outgrowth of the flexibility given to judges in the Federal Rules of Evidence to admit or exclude testimony based on their own discretion.

According to the Court in *Daubert*, "scientific" focuses on the methods and procedures of science, while "knowledge" focuses on objective beliefs or supported evidence. The intent of the Court in providing greater flexibility is further evident in its decision to focus on the principles and methodology of the expert's testimony, rather than on the conclusions. However, the decision as to if, which, and how the factors are to be used was left to the discretion of the judge.

Standards for Reliability and Relevance

The testimony of expert witnesses is intended to clarify and interpret facts so the jury can understand the relevant scientific or technical information and thereby render a decision. Federal Rule of Evidence 702 states that reliable expert testimony must be based on scientific fact and not subjective belief or opinion. Rule 702 further requires that a valid scientific relationship needs to be established between the evidence to be offered and the issue to be tried. If this relationship can be reasonably established, the expert testimony is admissible as evidence. Testimony that is not relevant does not assist the jury in better understanding the evidence or in ultimately rendering a just verdict.

Daubert suggested two additional considerations for determining the admissibility of expert testimony. The first concerns the extent to which the theory or technique used in the expert testimony relies on the expert's subjective interpretation. The testifying expert must show that the basis for his or her testimony is objective. This can be established by presenting peer-reviewed literature showing that the evidence is based on unbiased and objective methodology, logic, and assumptions. Additionally, the expert's field of expertise must be recognized as a reliable discipline among other experts, regardless of degrees and experience.

The second consideration concerns the application of the theory or technique outside the context of litigation. In the case of a new theory, the expert must establish that it can be objectively substantiated through independent testing or application.

The Role of the Judge under *Daubert*

Daubert established the role of the trial judge as "gatekeeper" for the admission of expert evidence and testimony. This gatekeeper role guards the jury from considering evidence that was purely speculative but offered under the guise of legitimate, scientifically based expert opinion. Although judges are not expected to be scientists, they must demonstrate the ability to think like scientists. They must understand the philosophical and practical standards of scientific method. In cases of doubt or inordinate complexity, judges can engage experts in the field to help them understand and ultimately decide an issue, but judges make the final decision.

To successfully accomplish this role, judges have the general provisions of the Federal Rules of Evidence as well as the *Daubert* factors to rely on. The trial judge must first determine whether the witness is appropriately qualified to provide expert testimony. Second, the trial judge must provide an initial assessment as to the validity, reasoning, and underlying methodology upon which the expert's opinion is based. Finally, prior to admitting expert opinion and/or testimony, the trial judge must determine the extent to which the testimony or methodology fits the specific circumstances of the case. After considering these guiding principles, the trial judge is able to determine the reliability and relevance of expert testimony and then decide if it is admissible as evidence in the specific case to be tried.

The decision of the trial judge to admit or exclude expert testimony may come at various times in the litigation. During the pre-trial process, either party may file motions to exclude expert testimony by comparing expert opinions to the *Daubert* factors. In response to pretrial motions, the judge has several options. First, he or she can rule on the reliability, relevance, and admissibility of the proposed testimony based strictly upon the arguments of the attorneys and supporting material provided to the court. The court may also hold a hearing prior to trial where the expert must testify to matters that address the *Daubert* factors; this testimony is then considered along with the oral arguments. If the court wishes additional guidance, the judge may appoint independent experts to review the motions and make recommendations. The judge can also allow the case to proceed and decide during trial.

While the *Daubert* test provides the basis for challenging proposed expert testimony, trial judges can use, reject, or modify any of the *Daubert* factors at their own discretion. Because trial judges, unlike juries, have the opportunity to review and question expert testimony prior to trial, over time they may develop an understanding of science that potentially allows more prudent and accurate decisions, meaning they admit scientific evidence only when they are convinced of its validity and reliability. Of course, judges are susceptible to committing errors either by admitting invalid scientific evidence or excluding valid evidence. Ultimately, the key objective may be for the judge to weigh the harm of erring in admitting evidence versus the harm of erring in excluding evidence.

> Post-*Daubert* courts are admitting more scientific evidence in civil and criminal cases. When dealing with scientific evidence about which there is limited agreement in the scientific community, the disputes among scientists are replicated in the courtroom, and the trial judge has had to reconcile these genuine disagreements. The result of these gatekeeping exercises is a tortured landscape of post-*Daubert* decisions, which are non-uniform, inconsistent, and irreconcilable. When different courts are presented with the same scientific methodology, the depth of their scrutiny varies considerably and the gatekeeping factors are not applied uniformly. Not surprisingly, courts reach different and at times conflicting conclusions on admissibility.[1]

In the final analysis under *Daubert*, the trial judge is primarily responsible for ensuring that the jury is properly influenced by reliable and relevant testimony and not by impressive credentials or persuasive but unfounded arguments. "A hunch based on years of practical experience will not suffice."[2] *Daubert* emphasizes that the "focus of the trial judge's inquiry must be solely on principles and methodology, not on the conclusions that they generate. The substance of the conclusion should not be questioned by the trial judge. The trial judge only needs to determine whether the scope of the conclusion is in keeping with the methodology employed."[3]

Daubert serves both to limit as well as broaden the admissibility of evidence. While new and novel scientific theories and techniques not meeting the *Frye* "general acceptance" standard can be admissible under *Daubert*, the intent is still clearly to ensure that only testimony that is reliable and relevant be admitted and that "junk science" does not invade the court.

[1] Jay P. Kesan, A critical examination of the Post-*Daubert* scientific evidence landscape, *Georgetown Law Journal* (1996), 20.

[2] David G. Savage, Putting the brakes on junk analysis, *ABA Journal*, (May 1999), 38.

[3] Kesan, 18.

Daubert Applied

While *Daubert* has been applied in literally thousands of civil and criminal cases since 1993, the way in which *Daubert* is applied varies — sometimes widely — among jurisdictions. Some courts directly apply the *Daubert* factors as provided in the original decision, while others modify these factors and their use as deemed appropriate. For example, the First Circuit Court of Appeals stringently reviews experts' qualifications, citing the need for experts to be "well or impressively credentialed." In contrast, the Third Circuit stresses the issue of relevance, stating that requirements of *Daubert* constitute a standard for determining fit in addition to relevance alone. In yet another differing interpretation, the Second Circuit states that "an expert's report is not a talisman against summary judgment" and that the judge performs the role of gatekeeper at the summary judgment stage of a case in trial.[4]

Differing interpretations of *Daubert* are not restricted to how the standards are applied, but also exist according to the type of testimony or witness. The Fourth Circuit Court does not apply *Daubert* to experts whose conclusions are based on experience and training, rather than on methodology. The Fifth Circuit Court contends that *Daubert* is applicable only to the "knowledge" component of scientific knowledge. The Sixth Circuit adds another factor to *Daubert* which addresses experts' pre-litigation research, as opposed to research conducted for purposes of litigation. The Seventh Circuit states that scientists must stick to the same standards of intellectual strictness inside the courtroom that they do outside, even if their methods are not yet officially accepted and/or approved by their respective scientific communities. The Ninth Circuit looks at experts' methodology as well as their conclusions to determine the relevance of testimony, explaining that testing and error-rate factors do not apply when experts have not done original research. The Tenth Circuit "applies *Daubert* only in cases involving unique, untested, or controversial methodologies or techniques"[5] and not to experts' testimony that is based only on experience or training. The Eleventh Circuit, on the other hand, applies *Daubert* only to witnesses with scientific expertise, as a scientific expert relies on scientific principles, rather than skill or experience, to form opinions.[6]

Not all courts consider *Daubert* to be a step in the right direction. The District of Columbia Circuit, for example, believes that the threshold for admitting expert testimony has diminished due to *Daubert* and considers gatekeeping to be a check on an expert's subjective beliefs or unsupported

[4] Eric Pierson, *1999 Wiley witness update: New developments in personal injury litigation* (Frederick, MD: Aspen Law and Business, 1999), 14.
[5] Pierson, 54.
[6] Pierson.

speculation. This court further acknowledges that *Daubert* is limited in nature and agrees that experts' testimony should be admissible when the methodology is explained, survives cross-examination, and fits an issue in the case.[7]

The Impact of *Daubert* on Expert Witnessing

Regardless of how *Daubert* is interpreted or applied, its impact on expert witnessing has been profound. As previously noted, *Daubert* required that judges become effective consumers of science. This requirement extends to lawyers and expert witnesses as well. Expert witnesses have become a fixture in the modern American courtroom, involved in virtually every tort case filed. Because the outcome of a case often depends on the persuasiveness of expert testimony, the selection, preparation and presentation of experts are critically important for successful litigation.

Choosing an expert requires consideration of the following:

1. *Qualification.* First and foremost, an expert must be able to demonstrate specialized skill or knowledge acquired through an appropriate mix of experience or education. Recognized expertise in the subject can be credibly substantiated by the authoring of peer-reviewed papers and books, recognition by peers for contributions to the field over an extended period of time, or other relevant activities recognized and accepted by other experts in the field.
2. *Ability to Communicate.* To be effective, an expert witness must have the ability to clearly and persuasively explain and communicate complex theories and results through explanation, simplification, and clarification, and by giving examples and analogies.
3. *Litigation Experience.* Through actual litigation experience, experts learn what is expected of them as well as what to expect in the various steps of the litigation process. Additionally, lawyers are inclined to depend on experts who understand the litigation process and are able to withstand rigorous critique of their testimony by opposing attorneys hoping to discredit the expert.
4. *Commitment.* An expert must be able and willing to commit the time and energy needed to adequately conduct research and to formulate defensible opinions.
5. *Proximity.* Experts in the vicinity of the trial location are often more convenient and less expensive due to the absence of travel costs. On the other hand, experts from faraway places may be more impressive

[7] Pierson.

to a jury, particularly if the faraway place is a prestigious university or research institute.

6. *Cost.* The fee of an expert is a significant variable. A proven expert with a highly effective track record may cost more per hour, but may be far more attractive in terms of efficiency, effectiveness, and overall impact.

Most certainly, expert testimony must meet the *Daubert* standards for reliability and relevance. However, in contested cases, the scientific facts are usually exceedingly difficult to unravel. If the scientific facts were obvious, the case would more than likely have been settled with little difficulty. In the absence of all the facts, experts must make reasonable assumptions and extrapolate information upon which to base their judgments and opinions. As a consequence, their realities end up constituting the basis for challenging the admissibility of their opinions.

Experts must thoroughly review and consider the *Daubert* factors when preparing their opinions. Additionally, the expert's report and testimony, whether in deposition or a pretrial hearing, must clearly and explicitly cover how the expert has met each of the appropriate factors. Experts must use theories that have gravity. Experts must present literature, preferably peer-reviewed, supporting their theories or opinions and demonstrating that their opinions are scientifically based, rather than merely subjective. *Daubert* allows for flexibility in determining the relevance and reliability of expert testimony but at the same time provides the basis for challenging the substantiation and support of the same expert testimony.

A Word on Junk Science

What is junk science? At its worst, junk science is the willful manipulation of biased data, false or erroneous conclusions, and fraudulent methodology in the attempt to "scientifically" substantiate a point that, in reality, cannot be substantiated. At its best, junk science is science or theory that has not been subjected to the scientific method and therefore lacks defensible support in the scientific community. More often that not, however, "junk science" is a pejorative term leveled at novel or emerging scientific theory merely because it has not been thoroughly vetted in the scientific community, even though it is grounded in fundamental scientific principles.

The advancement of science relies on new, speculative theories that are contrary to the generally accepted science of the day. Novel theories and methodologies should not be summarily dismissed by judges just because they are labeled "junk" by opposing lawyers and experts, or because verification of the methodology is not complete. Judges must be careful not to let the adversarial system degrade respectable and quality work as a matter of course just because someone has called it "junk."

An Additional Impact of *Daubert* — The Amended Rules of Evidence

The adoption of the Federal Rules of Evidence in 1975, while addressing the admission of opinion evidence by a qualified expert in a scientific or technical field, provided no guidance to judges on how to evaluate the relevance or reliability of expert testimony. Although in *Daubert* the Supreme Court defined the gatekeeping role of the trial judge in determining both the relevance and the reliability of expert testimony before allowing its admission, the Rules of Evidence remained ambiguous. This left a loophole so that lawyers occasionally attempted to squeeze in the testimony of experts under Rule 701, which governs opinions offered by lay witnesses, rather than under Rule 702, which specifically applies to scientific and technical experts. Opinion-based lay testimony was admissible so long as it was rationally based on the personal perception of the witness and was helpful to the trier of fact. The standards under Rule 701 differ greatly from those governing expert testimony under Rule 702.

This loophole was not closed until the Rules were amended in 2000. The amended Rule 701 reads as follows: "If the witness is not testifying as an expert, the witness's testimony in the form of opinions or inferences is limited to those opinions or inferences which are (a) rationally based on the perception of the witness, (b) helpful to a clear understanding of the witness's testimony or the determination of a fact in issue, and (c) not based on scientific, technical, or other specialized knowledge within the scope of Rule 702."

It is important to note that the amended rule "does not distinguish between expert and lay witnesses, but rather between expert and lay testimony."[8] The rules governing traditional lay witness testimony remain unchanged. In certain circumstances, it is possible that the same witness could provide both expert and lay testimony in the same case. In this event, the lay testimony would be covered by Rule 701, and the expert testimony would be covered by the more stringent Rule 702.[9]

The most significant amendment was made to Federal Rule of Evidence 702, the rule that expressly governs expert testimony. The new rule, which

[8] Daniel J. Capra, Evidence rules receive changes effective December 1: Part 2, LRP Publications: *Federal Discovery News*, (December 11, 2000).
[9] Capra, 2.

became effective on December 1, 2000, now reads: "If scientific, technical, or other specialized knowledge will assist the trier of fact to understand the evidence or to determine a fact in issue, a witness qualified as an expert by knowledge, skill, experience, training, or education may testify thereto in the form of an opinion or otherwise, if (1) the testimony is based upon sufficient facts or data, (2) the testimony is the product of reliable principles and methods, and (3) the witness has applied the principles and methods reliably to the facts of the case."

This amendment both reinforced and codified the *Daubert* principles as well as helped to clarify the ambiguities of *Daubert* that had been illustrated through conflicting decisions in trial courts. The gatekeeping role of the judge to ensure that testimony is both relevant and reliable is clearly reinforced. Consistent with the objective of *Daubert* to exclude unreasonable and unfounded expert testimony, the amended rule also establishes general guidance for trial courts to use in their evaluation. Additionally, Rule 702 now specifically extends the *Daubert* gatekeeping role of the trial judge to all expert testimony, in accordance with the Supreme Court decision in *Kumho*.

In an attempt to provide clarity, and therefore uniformity, in the application of *Daubert* in another area of division, amended Rule 702 addresses experience as a basis for expert qualification. Note 47 to Rule 702 states, "if the witness is relying solely or primarily on experience, then the witness must explain how that experience leads to the conclusions reached, why that experience is a sufficient basis for the opinion, and how that experience is reliably applied to the facts."[10]

The Rules also address the sources upon which experts may base their testimony. Rule 703 permits an expert to rely on information that is not admissible at trial, such as hearsay evidence, so long as it is "of a type reasonably relied upon by experts in the particular field in forming opinions or inferences upon the subject." While experts may still rely upon facts and data that might not be admissible in evidence, the amended Rule 703 prohibits disclosure of otherwise inadmissible data unless the court determines that the value of the evidence to the jury in understanding the expert's opinion substantially outweighs the potential for bias or prejudice. This change essentially eliminated the ability of an attorney to present normally inadmissible evidence through the testimony of an expert witness in the form of supporting data. The amended rule closed the loophole of its use as a *de facto* hearsay exception.

Rule 704, the rule that governs opinion testimony, was also amended. The amendment to this rule states that: "(a) Except as provided in subdivision (b), testimony in the form of an opinion or inference otherwise admissible

[10] Stephen S. McCloskey, Recent developments in civil procedure and evidence, *Tort and Law Journal* (Winter 2001), 6.

is not objectionable because it embraces an ultimate issue to be decided by the trier of fact. (b) No expert witness testifying with respect to the mental state or condition of a defendant in a criminal case may state an opinion or inference as to whether the defendant did or did not have the mental state or condition constituting an element of the crime charge or of a defense thereto. Such ultimate issues are for the trier of fact alone."

Rule 705 was amended to allow an expert to provide his or her opinion without disclosing any underlying facts or data. Subject to the discretion of the trial judge, the examining lawyer can decide how or whether to reveal an expert's opinions. Essentially, Rule 705 permits a qualified expert to provide opinions and conclusions before revealing any other information.[11]

Finally, the December 2000 amendments gave new strength to the little-used rule governing court-appointed experts. Federal Rule of Evidence 706 allows federal courts to appoint their own expert witnesses. While the parties involved in the litigation may be asked to submit nominations, the trial judge retains discretion in the choice and use of court-appointed experts, including the authority to inform the jury that an expert has been court appointed.

Many states have adopted the Federal Rules of Evidence or a close approximation, such as the Uniform Rules of Evidence (1999), in an attempt to ensure uniformity between federal and state judicial proceedings. However, in reality, consensus between federal and state rules continues to be elusive. Beyond the expected differences in interpretation, there is an increasing tendency among state courts to reject the guidance provided in *Daubert* and the subsequent clarifying cases. Many states, including Florida, Maryland, New Jersey, New York, and Pennsylvania, decline to follow *Daubert* in its entirety.

Without question, the Federal Rules of Evidence have undergone several significant changes following the United States Supreme Court *Daubert* decision. Though several cases have clarified or extended the four factors outlined in the landmark ruling, the *Daubert* standard still provides the primary basis for determining the reliability of expert testimony in the federal judicial system, with a primary intent to exclude opinions that do not meet the threshold for scientific validity.

[11] Justin P. Murphy, Expert witnesses at trial: Where are the ethics? *The Georgetown Journal of Legal Ethics* (Fall 2000), 217–239.

Section II

The Litigation Process

May you have a lawsuit in which you know you are in the right.

—Gypsy Proverb

4

The Pre-Trial Process

I can't do literary work for the rest of this year because I'm meditating another lawsuit and looking around for a defendant.

—Mark Twain

In most cases, the first formal notice of a lawsuit is the complaint. This is a legal document written in very general terms alleging some cause of action, i.e., the way a party has been harmed. An example might be a breach of contract in which one party did not perform agreed-upon items. Another cause of action is negligence, in which one party violated the standard of care in the fulfillment of an obligation.

Affirmative Defenses

Provided there are no objections to the complaint, the opposing party files an answer. In a typical answer, all claims are denied and so-called affirmative defenses are presented. An affirmative defense is a legal basis to bar a plaintiff from recovery, even if the allegations in the complaint are true. Affirmative defenses refer to legal grounds for dismissal, as opposed to factual grounds.

Common affirmative defenses are waiver, assumption of the risk, and statute of limitations. A waiver is an action by the plaintiff that results in giving up the claim. For example, a plaintiff waives the right to sue by signing a settlement agreement before initiating litigation. A plaintiff assumes the risk of injury by knowingly engaging in an act that will likely cause injury, such as hang gliding, cliff diving, or other extreme sports. The defense of statute of limitations refers to the expiration of the legally established time limit for asserting a claim.

In addition to affirmative defenses, a defendant may assert a claim against the plaintiff or another party. A claim made by the defendant against the plaintiff is called a counterclaim. Third-party claims involve shifting the responsibility to another party. The defendant states that he or she was not responsible but rather a different party — the third party — was. For example, a third-party claim could involve the shift of responsibility from the prime contractor to a subcontractor. For any affirmative defense or third-party claim, the burden of proof resides with the defendant.

Complaints, affirmative defenses, and counterclaims combine to create the pleadings in a case and define the legal issues, factual contentions, and theories of relief or defense. Pleadings must be specific enough to substantiate litigation without dismissal, while at the same time broad and ambiguous enough to allow for amending or fine-tuning claims and defenses as the litigation unfolds.

The expert can be helpful to the attorney in constructing the complaint, in developing the answer and affirmative defenses, or identifying additional parties who should be included in the lawsuit.

Discovery

Once all the pleadings have been filed, the next stage of a lawsuit is discovery. Discovery is the formal pretrial process of fact-finding in which lawyers from both sides are able to obtain facts and information about the opposing party's case. During discovery, each party gives the opposing party access to information, documents, and key witnesses with pertinent facts. A primary purpose of discovery is to ensure that cases are decided based on the evidence known in advance, rather than as a result of surprises in the courtroom. Attorneys from both sides use the information provided during discovery to develop their strategies for trying the case.

Discovery is comprised of three primary parts: interrogatories, requests for production of documents, and depositions. Rule 26(b)(4) of the Federal Rules of Civil Procedure establishes a two-stage discovery process for testifying experts. The first stage outlines what the parties must do, such as respond to interrogatories; provide pertinent documents; identify experts, their subject matter, and the substance of their facts or opinions; and provide a summary of the grounds for each fact or opinion. The second stage allows the court to order further discovery by other means. This process may be subject to the payment of fees in certain circumstances. Beyond this, however, there are really few clear ground rules.

The intent of discovery is to gather information and facts relevant to the case. While the scope of discovery is broader than the scope of admissible evidence in trial, unreasonably broad requests for information, sometimes called "fishing expeditions,"[1] are not allowed. Requests cannot be overly broad or cause undue burden on the party answering them. Information must be relevant and must lead to the discovery of admissible evidence.

Cases can be won or lost during discovery. Sometimes key information is never properly requested from the other side; key documents may not be identified or, conversely, there may be so many documents that they cannot be properly tracked or inspected. To be successful as an expert witness, you must know the strategy and tactics required to organize yourself and your information most effectively. Courts encourage both sides to become knowledgeable about the facts and relative value of their positions in the hope that a settlement can be reached prior to trial. In the event that the case does go to trial, proper discovery and preparation can expedite the case. As a result, discovery is often the most time-consuming aspect of litigation, in some cases lasting years.

Interrogatories

Interrogatories are a common form of written discovery and are comprised of a series of written questions sent to the opposing party. Upon receipt, the receiving party has thirty days in which to respond or raise objection to any or all of the written questions received. Objections may be based upon grounds that reflect the burden on the answering party. Additionally, parties can claim that the information or documents are subject to the attorney-client privilege and therefore may not be released to the opposing party. The trial judge ultimately decides whether any of the objections are valid.

Interrogatories are directed to the parties themselves. Responses must be in writing and signed by the party under oath. In addition to getting factual information about a party's claims or defenses, interrogatories can be used to gain information about the scientific foundation of the opposing side's case, including the identification of expert witnesses who will testify and the subject matter of their expected testimony.

[1] Thomas A. Hunter, Some hazards of being an expert witness, Paper presented at *The American Society of Mechanical Engineers* (November 8–13, 1992), 5

Experts should assist in both developing and drafting interrogatories. Based upon their expertise, experts are often in the best position to determine whether the information requested is scientifically or technically relevant and if it either indicates or fits within a strategy for the case. Often, experts identify the vulnerabilities of the expert testimony provided by the opposing side. These vulnerabilities, whether stemming from questions of fact, methodology, reliability, or relevancy, can be exploited during cross-examination to undermine the opposing side's case. Identifying the right questions and giving thorough responses during the interrogatory process can greatly enhance the defensibility of expert testimony.

The interrogatory process can be both burdensome and expensive. Lawyers can use the interrogatory process to wear down the opposition by requesting inordinate amounts of information from virtually anyone remotely associated or involved with the case. In 1993, Rule 26 of the Federal Rules of Civil Procedure was amended to limit both the number of interrogatories a party may propound to twenty-five, including subparts, and the number of depositions to ten. Under certain circumstances, the court may allow additional interrogatories or depositions, as long as the process complies with the rules of discovery; the process is not unduly burdensome, duplicative or expensive; and the benefits outweigh the costs involved. "Part of the reasoning behind the amendment was that much of the information ordinarily covered in a traditional first set of interrogatories should now be covered by the automatic disclosure provisions of Rule 26(a)."[2]

Automatic Disclosure

The Federal Rules of Civil Procedure now contain automatic disclosure provisions. Rule 26(a)(1) requires that each party provide to the other the following information without waiting for a discovery request:

- the names and addresses of all witnesses and the subject matter on which they have information
- a list of all relevant documents, data, or other tangible information relevant to the proceedings which the party has in its possession
- any and all damages claimed, including the basis upon which they were calculated

[2] Michael E. Sacks, *An overview of the law: A guide for testifying and consulting experts* (Horsham, PA: LRP Publications, 1995), 13.

In addition, many federal and state jurisdictions ask for an expert disclosure, either with or without deposition. The expert disclosure can take a variety of forms; in most cases, it must follow specific guidelines and be signed by the expert and notarized.

The automatic disclosure provisions are intended to streamline the discovery process, to eliminate abuse and excessive cost, and to encourage early and full disclosure of relevant information regarding the case.[3] Whether to adopt the automatic disclosure provisions is at the discretion of individual federal district courts; state courts may or may not have civil rules of procedure that mirror the federal rule. As a result, this rule is not fully adopted in all federal and state jurisdictions.

Production of Documents

In the discovery process, any party may serve any other parties with a request for the production of documents which seeks all written material relevant to the specific subject of the litigation. As in the case of interrogatories, a party served with a request to produce documents has thirty days to respond by producing all of the documents requested, by notifying the requesting party of the arrangements made to produce all of the documents requested, or by filing a specific legal objection to part or all of the request.[4] In support of this effort, an effective expert needs to educate the lawyer on the types of documents that are available and that are most likely to provide the best insight into the case and the opposing party's position.

The production of documents in federal cases is governed by Rule 34. This rule states that parties requesting documents can inspect or make copies of documents or obtain access to information stored in electronic form, including printouts. This applies to all types of documents, including correspondence, drawings, graphs, charts, photographs, phone records, test results, laboratory reports, and other data compilations. The rule may also apply to preliminary drafts, working papers, handwritten notes, and personal diaries, as long as they contain relevant information that is not classified as privileged.[5]

While most documents and records are subject to production, some that are classified as privileged are protected and therefore need not be produced. Privileged information falls within the following three categories:

[3] Sacks.
[4] Sacks.
[5] Sacks.

1. *Attorney-Client Privilege.* Communications between a client and his or her attorney during the course of representation are not discoverable.
2. *Work Product Privilege.* Documents prepared in anticipation of litigation under the supervision or at the direction of an attorney are not discoverable. Working papers under the direction of an attorney, such as notes of telephone conversations, are also exempt from discovery. But be careful what you write. Some work product documents can be discovered, such as calculations that can and most probably will be introduced as evidence. Also, there are times the judge will require you to produce documents if the information is no longer available from another source. You may have the only copy of an important drawing, for example. If you are designated a testifying expert at some point, you may be required to produce all work product. Unless you are retained specifically as a consulting expert and are not expected to testify, assume that your work product will be discoverable.
3. *Proprietary Processes and Patents Privilege.* Information that is vulnerable to exposure to competitors may be exempt, or it may be subject to production under a protective order issued by the court. You can be of great assistance to the lawyer in understanding what is and is not proprietary.

Questions about privilege are dealt with by the judge *in camera*. Through this process, only the judge reviews the material (in secret) before issuing a ruling on the validity of the claim of privilege.

Defense law firms often employ feast-or-famine discovery tactics. When the "feast" strategy is used, boxes and boxes of documents are produced. Most of the material is of little or no interest, creating a document bottleneck that can inhibit valuable materials from being found. Conversely, when the "famine" strategy is employed, documents are produced to the other side only when they have been specifically requested, or if the court compels their disclosure.

In either case, obtaining any *useful* documents is the challenge. Obtaining judicial relief from burdensome discovery strategies is equally challenging. Judges prefer to allow cases to proceed with minimal court direction during the discovery phase, with the parties working out their differences. As an expert, you will most likely become involved in efforts to identify those documents that may have been withheld but are critical to the case or, alternatively, to sift through mounds of documents in search of a smoking gun. If you are successful, your value to the case will increase dramatically.

Organization of Documents

Complex civil cases may involve thousands of documents. Parties cannot simply throw together or mix up documents when responding to a production-of-document request. Rule 34(b) requires that documents either must be produced as they are kept in the normal course of business, or must be organized and labeled to correspond with the categories in the request. Additionally, documents considered undiscoverable — such as those containing privileged information — must be identified to the opposing parties so that they can be referenced in pretrial and trial proceedings and motions.

To keep track of documents, a law firm usually prepares an index of all discovery documents. In some cases, the court requires each side to provide such indexes. The index typically organizes documents by title, author, date, and, in some cases, by "Bates" number.[6] Because a series of documents can consist of thousands of pages, a Bates number provides an easy reference for the attorney and the expert, facilitating communication about important documents or the organization of documents located in more than one location. The Bates numbering machine allows for a number and letter combination of up to seven characters to be stamped directly onto a document. Letter prefixes can be used to identify the party who produced the document. For example, documents produced by Smith may be stamped SM000001, etc.

The organization of material is critical to your effectiveness as an expert. You must make sure you have the information you need to form and support your opinion. You must make sure your documents are organized so you can retrieve and keep track of those that are critical — especially when you are being deluged with materials. Just knowing that a critical document is in one of your boxes of papers is not enough; you must be able to find it and tie it to other key documents.

One effective way to organize your documents is to keep a computer database that identifies the documents by key information, such as date, source, subject matter, and Bates number. Once you have this information, you can then reorganize your documents to fit the structure of your written opinion or to identify those documents that you expect may be the subject of a deposition. Your organization scheme may also help the attorneys to lay the technical foundation for your side of the case. This is precisely the information that your attorney may need to make additional discovery requests and to assist in taking the deposition of the opposing expert.

In order to establish and substantiate an objective opinion, you must identify sources of information in addition to those provided through discovery. Documents can be obtained from individuals or entities who are not

[6] A Bates number is a number affixed by a Bates number-stamping machine. The machine is named for its inventor.

directly involved with the litigation, such as regulatory agencies, trade associations, and vendors. Additionally, access to documents may be needed to analyze the condition of, or conduct testing on, an actual piece of evidence. You must take special care when disassembling or sampling a piece of physical evidence in order to preserve the item's integrity. It is important to remember that the rules of procedure likely will require you to produce every document created, relied upon, reviewed, or possessed during the case.

Chain of Custody

Chain of custody refers to the ability to (a) establish the existence of a piece of evidence currently within a person's possession, custody, or control and (b) illustrate the safeguards taken to preserve the condition of the evidence while in that person's control or possession. This is extremely important to avoid the possibility that critical evidence is ruled inadmissible because it was not properly safeguarded to ensure its condition and resultant validity. If evidence has been altered, it may be excluded from being introduced, and testimony concerning that evidence may be barred. If the piece of evidence is central to the case, there is a risk that the entire case will be dismissed. Unintentional alteration of evidence can result in unpredictable outcomes and challenges. Intentional alteration is a criminal offense.

It is advantageous to carefully photograph, label, and register evidence — documents and physical evidence alike. For safety, evidence should be photographed in its current location prior to being moved to a new location. Certified or registered mail should be used when mailing evidence. A registered and bonded courier service should be used to transfer evidence within local areas when mail is either inappropriate or inconvenient. When not needed, evidence should be securely stored and locked. A chain-of-custody log, complete with records and notes as to what is being done with the evidence, must be established and maintained.[7]

In some cases, tests and/or experiments must be conducted in order to establish an opinion or to test the contention of another expert. Such tests can involve the use of physical evidence. In order to avoid spoliation as a result of testing it, the expert should consider the following:

1. Work closely with the attorney who engaged you. Frankly explain the types of tests to be performed, if and how the product may likely function differently after testing, and whether all or any part of the evidence will be altered or destroyed in the course of testing.

[7] Sacks.

2. Determine if any relevant professional organizations have testing protocols applicable to the testing to be conducted. If so, inform the attorney of such protocols and the advisability of following them to ensure that the testing will stand up to scrutiny on cross-examination.
3. Document the testing process and results with photographs and/or videotape.
4. Do not throw away anything you use in the course of forming your opinion, at least until the case has been settled or a final decision has been rendered. Even then, you or the attorney may need the material and/or evidence in the future. If in doubt, keep it.
5. Anticipate potential questions that might be asked on cross-examination about the testing process and address those issues before or during testing.
6. If testing that may result in the destruction of evidence is unavoidable, advise the attorney to consider bringing in the other side's expert for joint testing and/or observation.[8]

Joint testing results in "neutralizing the process,"[9] since both parties can observe and participate in the process together, reducing the possibility of suspicion. Arguments concerning mishandled and/or destroyed evidence are alleviated. Unfortunately, and despite the apparent advantages, joint testing of evidence is not the norm.

Experiments may be crucial to your opinion and should be pursued if that is the case. Experiments can be introduced as evidence only if the evidence is material and relevant, and if there is a tangible resemblance between conditions present when the actual event happened and when the experiment was conducted. Some courts are reluctant to admit experiments as evidence. With or without the attorneys involved, experts alone are expected to handle evidence in accordance with scientific, technical, and legal standards and to properly maintain the chain of custody. Remember that test work is subject to the *Daubert* criteria, particularly with respect to methodology and testing protocol.

The Expert Report

As previously discussed in Chapter 1, there are two kinds of experts — those who consult and those who testify. Generally speaking, the consulting expert provides background knowledge, while the testifying witness provides testimony in support of the party's claims in depositions, hearings, or trials. While

[8] Sacks.
[9] Sacks, 37.

the distinction between the two is fairly straightforward, the rules governing disclosure of information by the two are both substantially and significantly different, depending on the jurisdiction. This difference is especially important in its implications for the expert report.

The identities of experts who are informally consulted and retained but who will not testify are protected by law, as are their reports and other work product. In most jurisdictions, the work of the consulting expert is privileged and therefore not discoverable except in exceptional circumstances, or unless it is directly used or referred to in testimony, while the work of a testifying witness is discoverable, in accordance with Rule 26 of the Federal Rules of Civil Procedure. Because the opposing attorney does not want to be forced to reveal his or her consultant or the consultant's findings, the attorney may avoid seeking the identity and findings of the proponent's consulting expert. "The safer course is to treat a non-testifying expert just like the testifying expert until a firm decision is made that the nontestifying expert shall never see the shadowy light of the courtroom."[10]

An expert report is a formal written document that contains a testifying expert's credentials, opinions, the basis for those opinions, and conclusions to be offered at trial. The expert report must be prepared and signed by the expert unless otherwise directed by the trial judge. In cases that are highly complex and that evolve over a long period of time, an expert may be required to write a preliminary report, a report, and then a supplementary report. Most often, the need for a supplementary expert report arises in cases that require a preliminary report early in the proceedings when little information is available, or where the expert changes his or her opinion or conclusions based on newly discovered material or errors.

The information relied on to develop an expert report is discoverable and must be made available to the other side. Consequently, an expert should not write any reports or drafts of reports unless instructed to do so by his or her lawyer. Draft reports can be discoverable and presented as evidence in court. Drafts could be used in court against experts who wrote them because they might demonstrate weaknesses and ambiguities prior to developing the final report. Many experts have document destruction policies so that drafts are either copied over in the computer or shredded. Experts and attorneys should discuss draft reports in person or over the phone.

It is wise, however, to begin thinking about the report even before it is requested. The expert can begin identifying and organizing information needed to develop the expert opinion, including advice from the attorneys working on the case. An expert needs to fully grasp what subject matter is involved and the potential scope of any opinions. To accomplish this,

[10] David M. Malone and Paul J. Zwier, *Effective expert testimony* (Notre Dame, IN: National Institute for Trial Advocacy, 2000), 34.

attorneys should give the expert a general outline of the issues involved in the case and also explore associated avenues that experts might consider in the development of their opinions and the expert report.

The ultimate test of an expert report is the successful withstanding of a *Daubert* motion to exclude the expert's opinions.

Preparing the Expert Report

Because of the scope of permissible discovery under Federal Rule of Civil Procedure 26, you should limit written correspondence between you and your lawyer, and only provide your lawyer with a draft opinion upon request, especially if you are a testifying expert. Your attorney will advise you when any written documents and/or opinions are necessary. Your attorney will also advise you whether your documents need to comply with the federal rules of expert disclosure or any other specific form or format for presentation to the court. You should remember that once a report or other document has been written, it is subject to disclosure. Information you relied upon to develop your opinion is most likely also discoverable. Papers, articles, memos, calculations, and facts you used to prepare your expert report must be made available to the other side.[11]

Rule 26(a)(2) requires that any expert who may be presented at trial must be identified beforehand and that a signed report must be provided. This rule was amended in 1993 to address the specific minimum content for an export report. Rule 26 (a)(2) states:

> The report shall contain a complete statement of all opinions to be expressed and the basis and reasons therefore; the data or other information considered by the witness in forming the opinions; any exhibits to be used as a summary of or support for the opinions; the qualifications of the witness, including a list of all publications authored by the witness within the preceding ten years; the compensation to be paid for the study and testimony; and a listing of any other cases in which the witness has testified as an expert at trial or by deposition within the preceding four years.[12]

In addition, most states have specific deadlines by which an attorney must disclose the expert's report.

The whole point of the report is to give the opposing attorney the proper information and the opportunity to prepare for and counter your opinions

[11] John P. Coniglio, The expert witness: A primer on your activities, *Professional Safety* (January 2002), 34–39.
[12] Sacks, 16–17.

with other expert opinions and evidence. The 1993 changes not only made the filing of expert reports mandatory in federal court cases, but also changed the way expert testimony is accepted by the court. Experts must include all facts and conclusions in their written report because what they include in those pages will dictate what is allowed in their oral testimony. Supplemental reports can be written by an expert and submitted after the main report so that the expert can elaborate on specific issues new to the case. This approach allows experts to respond to new information. The most important thing is to get all the information out on the table so that there are no surprises.

A well-done, professional expert report should include the following items:

- Your qualifications
- The client's name and address
- The client's attorney's name and address
- A general description of the subject
- The objective
- The general methodology
- A summary of the conclusions
- Specifics of the investigation
- Demonstrative evidence such as photographs, maps, charts, and summaries
- Investigative reports incorporated in your report
- Test examinations, calculations, or other procedures you followed
- Consultation with other experts
- A statement of various hypotheses under investigation
- Areas of investigation still open due to unavailability of data or incomplete test or evaluation results
- Findings on physical examination
- Treatment, remedies, or corrective action, including what was done and methods followed
- Limiting conditions, exclusions, and disclaimers; you may wish to qualify your opinion or leave the conclusion somewhat open, subject to later determined facts.[13]

Deposition

Depositions are sworn testimonies given before trial by all potential witnesses, experts, and parties involved in the litigation.[14] The purpose of the

[13] How to make your written report work for you, *The Testifying Expert* (January 1996), 4.
[14] Marc A. Rabinoff and Stephen P. Holmes, *The forensic expert's guide to litigation: The anatomy of a lawsuit* (Horsham, PA: LRP Publications, 1996).

deposition process "is to gather information — not to try the case."[15] Although no judge is present, the witness is sworn by a court reporter to tell the truth, and a transcript of the testimony is prepared. Depositions provide the best, most direct way to closely define the bases of expert opinions and to characterize the background and expertise of the witness.

Under Federal Rules of Civil Procedure Rule 26 (b)(4)(A) the deposition of an expert is to be taken after the expert report has been completed and reviewed by parties from both sides and all supporting information has been identified. The deposition transcript becomes a written record by which an expert or witness can be impeached if the testimony varies between the deposition and the trial. If there are multiple expert reports, there can be multiple depositions. The other side has the right to depose an expert whenever opinions change or new facts are added to the existing opinions and a supplemental report is filed.

There are two kinds of depositions: discovery and evidentiary. Discovery depositions are taken by the opposing party to learn what the witness has to say. Evidentiary depositions are taken to record and thereby preserve a witness's testimony for use at trial. Evidentiary depositions are most often videotaped. (Generally, an expert will be notified in advance if the deposition is to be videotaped.) These depositions resemble trial testimony, where a lawyer conducts a full direct examination followed by the opposing attorney's cross-examination. In this situation, an expert or witness is expected to dress, act, and answer as if he or she were actually in the courtroom. Again, it is important to remember that all or part of any deposition, whether discovery or evidentiary, could be introduced at trial. Always assume that the deposition will be very difficult and that you need to be fully prepared to justify your opinions.

Depositions can be minor skirmishes or major battlefields, depending on how the discovery material is utilized, and are often used to set the tone for the case. Depositions are greatly influenced by the rest of the discovery process and can be more important than trial, since most cases settle and never get to the courtroom. What is said in the deposition and how it is said can establish the foundation for settlement negotiations and mediation.

The scope of questions at a deposition can be much broader than at trial. In a deposition, an opposing attorney may take greater risks in the questions posed — even knowing that an adverse answer may result – in order to gain clearer insight into the opposing position and the relative strength of that position. Most cases are settled after all depositions are taken and both sides are fully familiar with all the issues. Theoretically, reasonable people can, at that time, arrive at mutually agreeable terms. The presiding judge may be

[15] Hunter, 1.

leaning heavily on the parties to settle, working to eliminate cases from a crowded docket (calendar).

As an expert, you can be an asset to a lawyer during the depositions of other witnesses. You can better understand the nuances of the testimony, identify questions for the lawyer to ask in the deposition, or simply provide reactions concerning the information or evidence provided. Further, you can study the personalities involved in order to help create a strategy for cross-examination, should the case proceed to trial.

The attorneys arrange for the time and place of the deposition. Effort is made to ensure that the arrangements are convenient to the experts involved, but there are no guarantees. In the event that agreement on time and place cannot be reached, a formal notice of deposition, subpoena, or court order can be issued. Failure to appear at deposition can result in a number of different sanctions, such as monetary penalties or, in the worst case, exclusion of the expert's testimony.

A subpoena is a legal order that can be used to compel a witness to appear at a deposition or trial. If subpoenaed, a witness cannot decline to testify. Practically speaking, two types of subpoenas are associated with expert witnesses. The simple subpoena is a summons directing you to appear at a particular time and place and to testify as a witness. The second type, a subpoena *duces tecum,* is most commonly used for expert witnesses because it not only requires attendance and testimony but also requires that specified materials, files, and documents be brought to the deposition. A subpoena often includes a small amount of money, usually between $1 and $50 that serves as the fee for appearing. The geographical boundaries in which a subpoena may be served are determined by the law of the governing jurisdiction. A subpoena must be served on the witness personally by an authorized person, such as a constable or process server. Generally, however, the attorney for the expert negotiates the time and place of the deposition with information supplied by the expert as to willingness to travel and open dates. The subpoena is usually sent to the law firm retaining the expert and then transmitted to the expert.

Preparing for a Deposition

Preparation for a deposition is different than preparation to testify at trial. To be most effective, you must know the difference. Certainly, in preparing for a deposition, you must be knowledgeable of the technical aspects within your expertise as they relate to the case. Additionally, you must have a complete grasp of materials, pleadings, interrogatories, documents, depositions of other witnesses, and any other material supplied by the attorney. You must be able to express your opinion and to provide the professional, academic, or research foundation supporting it. An articulated, substantiated, and thorough deposition can vastly contribute to an amicable and expedient settlement.

You must also be psychologically prepared. It is imperative that you understand the theme of the case, as well as the strategies to be employed by the attorneys and the part that the expert is expected to play. You may discuss ahead of time with the attorneys the type of questions to be asked in the deposition. Practice how to appropriately answer open-ended and "help me" questions without falling into the traps that opposing lawyers may set.

Do not be reluctant to answer questions about your fees or compensation. You are being paid for your expertise and your time — just like the people asking you the questions. What you are being paid has no bearing on the outcome of the trial. Remember that you are an expert in your area and are therefore more knowledgeable than the opposing attorney about that area. If you are honest and clear, and if you have prepared yourself well on what to expect in both the tactics and the strategy of the opposing case, you should feel ready as you walk into the deposition.

The Process of Deposing Expert Witnesses

The rest of this chapter is intended to give you an idea of what to expect during a deposition and how to handle the process.

The Subpoena

You will likely receive a *subpoena duces tecum* from the attorney. This formalizes the date, time, and place of your deposition and outlines the substance of what you need to bring. The list is usually extensive, calling for practically everything you have written or done. You need to bring the relevant documents. Your attorney needs to give you direction on how to handle document production in a way that both is reasonable and honors the subpoena. It is also a good idea to ask your attorney before the beginning of the deposition about any stipulations or agreements between the two parties that might have an impact on your testimony.

If you have a good reason for not being able to show up at the deposition, you need to contact your attorney to reschedule. This can be done if you are ill, in another concurrent legal proceeding, called away on an emergency, or unavailable because of a very important unforeseen commitment. The deposition should have been scheduled at your convenience in the first place; changing it is usually not difficult if not done at the last minute or under a tight discovery deadline.

The Setting

The place of the deposition is negotiable. It can be set for the convenience of the expert, but it is usually held in the law offices of one of the attorneys. Anywhere from three to twenty people will be seated around the conference table, depending on how many parties are involved. Typically the court stenographer will set up equipment at one end of the table, and, if called for, the videographer will set up at the other end. Enter the room and introduce yourself. Sit down next to the stenographer. Your attorney will sit on the other side of you. The lead questioning attorney will sit across the table in your line of sight. In addition to the attorneys, you may find that clients and other experts are in the room to listen.

Before the deposition starts, the lawyers may banter among themselves informally. Do not engage them, and do not get caught up in their congeniality. Don't be misled by the informal atmosphere; this is a very serious proceeding.

Once everyone is seated and ready, the deposition starts with the stenographer asking you to take the standard oath. The lawyers will then explain the format and rules of the deposition and ask you to acknowledge your understanding of the process. Then the questions begin. The court reporter records everything that is said on the record.

The Opposing Attorney's Intent

Opposing attorneys normally depose experts after all other preparatory work has been completed and before the trial date. The deposition can be harder than the trial. It is hard because you have no control over the questioning process and may only answer the questions asked. The opposing attorney is in control. He or she may not be particularly interested in how well qualified you are, or what a great job you did to arrive at your opinions. The opposing attorney's job is to size you up and, if possible, set you up for a *Daubert* motion to exclude you as a witness or to impeach your testimony at trial. Attorneys test your and their own theories during depositions as they explore alternative story lines in preparation for trial. Depositions allow them to test how well these theories work in order to determine which ones can be developed at trial. Attorneys might use your deposition to gather bits and pieces of testimony to prepare motions unrelated to your actual work.

The opposing attorney has multiple goals in questioning you. The goals, in order of importance, are:

1. *Impeachment.* The attorney will be searching for inconsistencies, contradictions, and mistakes in your work. No work is perfect, and shortcomings may show up in yours. As the attorney approaches a weakness of yours, he or she has a choice: (a) Bore in on it, make you fully aware, and try to make you look foolish, even getting you to unwittingly admit your weaknesses, or (b) Try to get what he or she wants and then back off without fully revealing to you how important the issue is and save it for trial. One positive aspect of the questioning process is that you get to learn how much the opposing attorney knows and where he or she thinks you are vulnerable. This is good information that may give you direction about preparing for trial.
2. *Daubert Challenge.* The attorney will ask a string of questions directly related to the "relevance and reliability" test. You have the opportunity with each question to root your answer in one or several of the *Daubert* guidelines. Take advantage of it. Show how your methodology satisfies the general acceptance criteria and is good science. Have answers for the "error rate" questions. Affirmative, prepared responses are essential.
3. *Background.* Every witness has background issues. An academic person may not have worked extensively in industry or other non-academic setting. A practitioner may not have a strong academic grounding. The attorney will explore these areas, plus look for blank spaces on your resumé. You may have flunked out of college at one time or failed a professional exam. The attorney may attempt to temporarily damage your self-esteem by focusing on these matters. Do not be embarrassed by these questions or your answers. Your best approach is to answer the questions directly without embellishment or excuse.
4. *Character/Bias.* The attorney wants to know how you react under pressure and uncertainty. You will be asked questions that appear to be off the wall or will attack your character. You may be asked if it is true that most of your expert witness work is for one side or the other, attempting to show that you are biased. Your answer needs to be businesslike and responsive. You can do work primarily for one side or the other without being biased. The opposing attorney will bring out any sign of bias and ask you to respond to the charge. Just respond in a straightforward manner. Emotions do not get recorded in the deposition transcript; only your words do. Be professional in your demeanor and responses. Take time if necessary to think about your responses before answering. Time may be noted but has little or no impact on your testimony.

5. *Fencing/"Freezing".*[16] Deposing attorneys may try to limit the extent of your testimony to certain parts — usually the weaker or vulnerable parts. By building a "fence"[17] around your testimony, they are able to limit what you can say at trial or your ability to elaborate later. Lawyers try to accomplish this by using funnel questioning techniques that begin with a broad, open question then become narrower and narrower as they proceed in order to learn what you know about the particular subject and your strategy. These techniques rely on short, controlling, leading questions. When this happens, it is critical to point out that your answers reflect the factors that occur to you at the time so that you preserve the opportunity to clarify or elaborate later. Also, you have the right and responsibility to answer any question to the fullest of your ability. Do not answer a question with a simple "yes" or "no" if further explanations are necessary.
6. *Stretching.* Experts find themselves at times stretched to their limits. Your attorneys would love it if you were competent to give opinions on all the technical aspects of the case; however, if you cross the boundary of your expertise, watch out. Do not stretch. Do not let your attorney stretch you for opinions beyond your expertise. Opposing lawyers enjoy baiting experts to stretch their opinions, thereby destroying their credibility. Do not try to look good or be more than you are in the deposition. Know where the boundary is in advance, and respond to "stretch" questions with "it is beyond my expertise." There is no harm in admitting that. On the other hand, do not overly constrain your expertise and thereby draw too restrictive a boundary.
7. *Endurance.* Lawyers may be used to long days of depositions, but you may not. The opposing attorneys may want to wear you out and then, in your moments of exhaustion and weakness, have you respond the way they want. Your counter is that your expression and body language is one of endurance, a stance that says to the opposing attorney, "However long it takes, I will stay." Make the attorney ask the right questions for information, but answer in a forthright manner. You can always ask that the question be repeated or rephrased if not clear.

Preparing for the *Daubert* Challenge

Even if you believe yourself to be an expert in your field, you can still find yourself on the receiving end of a *Daubert* challenge. However, if you can meet the following criteria, you are more likely to survive a challenge:

[16] Steven Lubet, *Expert testimony: A guide for expert witnesses and the lawyers who examine them* (Boston: National Institute for Trial Advocacy, 1998), 144.
[17] Faust F. Rossi, *Expert Witnesses* (Chicago: American Bar Association, 1991), 163.

- Special training and/or education related to the area of expertise to be provided in the case
- Teaching experience related to the area of expertise to be provided in the case
- Work experience related to the area of expertise to be provided in the case
- Articles or books published on the area of expertise to be provided in the case
- Membership in professional organizations
- Number of times you have been consulted: where, when, and for whom
- Number of times you have testified: where, when, and for whom
- Fields in which you feel qualified and on what basis
- Knowledge and understanding of the seminal work or works in the area of expertise to be provided in the case
- Knowledge and understanding of the standard texts and/or references related to the area of expertise to be provided in the case
- Direct experience with the particular product or facts in issue
- Compensation[18]

A *Daubert* challenge can be a harrowing experience. In a recent case, for example, an expert used a standard, off-the-shelf software program to analyze data. Due to familiarity with the software from repeated use over time, he had identified several shortcomings and inefficiencies in the program, to which he made modifications. The modifications were reasonable and well-founded, and they resulted in both improved efficiency and accuracy of the program. Though the expert could easily explain them, he did not document the modifications that he made. The data that he used was accurate and sound, and the methodology he employed was also generally accepted within his field of expertise. However, because he made modifications to the software program that were (a) not documented, (b) not validated, and (c) not disclosed during discovery, he was rejected as an expert for the purpose of that trial.

Never prepare and/or document an opinion without considering the *Daubert* factors of relevance, reliability, and applicability. The best way to deal with *Daubert* is to cover the pertinent factors explicitly in your expert report. Have a section on the science, with literature cited. Discuss error rate. Show that your theory has been tested and is generally accepted. Explain the basis for assumptions. Your life as an expert witness will continue to become more difficult as a result of *Daubert*, but if you are constantly aware of the

[18] Richard T. Jones, Impeaching your opponent's expert, *The Brief* (Summer 1985).

guidelines, you will have a much greater likelihood of surviving the *Daubert* challenge. "No matter how majestic the qualifications are, they must match the subject matter of the testimony."[19]

Additional Pointers

- Never "volunteer" information. Use the number of words necessary to answer the question. If you need to elaborate, do so on a limited basis. Allow the examiner to extract additional information from you. Use "yes" or "no" answers when no elaboration is necessary. You are not in a deposition to lecture or show the breadth of your knowledge; you are there to be responsive to the questions and elaborate to the extent necessary to protect the record.
- *Take time to think before answering.* Pause after each question, even if you think you don't need to. You need to set the pace and control the timing of the process. Some attorneys like to control the pace of the deposition by using a rapid cadence and not allowing you to think before reacting. Do not let that happen. Conversely, do not take long pauses for no good reason. Gamesmanship is not necessary.
- *Make sure you understand the question.* If the question is not clear, too broad, or too complex, ask for a restatement or for further explanation. You can restate the question in your terms before answering.
- *Never guess at an answer.* Never guess at a question or answer before the entire question has been asked. You know what you know. If you do not know the answer, there are several ways to respond. You can explicitly say you do not know the answer. You can indicate that you cannot recall at that moment, but when, in the course of the deposition, you recall the information, you can let them know. You can say the question demands further research and that you will get back to them after a break. Never, never speculate in a deposition.
- *Never loose your cool.* Attorneys may test you by asking demeaning questions. Do not retaliate. Do not stand up and leave. Lawyers can be very good at provoking witnesses. Do not fall into that trap. Once they discover you are susceptible to emotional outbursts, they will have an advantage. Keep your emotions grounded and under control. Focus on what is being asked, rather than on how it is being asked.

[19] Eric Pierson, *1999 Wiley expert witness update: New development in personal injury litigation* (Frederick, MD: Aspen Law and Business, 1999), 139.

- *Finish your answers.* Lawyers will at times attempt to cut you off. You have the right and obligation to complete your statement. If cut off, respond that you need to finish the last question and do so prior to answering the next question.
- *Correct your answers.* If you misspoke on a previous question, revisit it and repair your answer before you leave the deposition.
- *Take time to review documents.* The attorney may offer a document as a formal exhibit. The stenographer will identify it with a number. You will then be asked to authenticate it. Look at it closely. If you recognize that you have already read the document, take time to refresh your memory. If you haven't read it previously, take the time to read it thoroughly before answering any question based on that document. Do not allow the attorney to rush you.
- *Cautiously answer hypothetical questions*: Lawyers may ask hypothetical questions based on assumptions intended to cast doubt on your opinion or conclusions. If you get caught up in answering such questions, you can damage your testimony. Only answer hypothetical questions if they contain the facts, circumstances, and conditions necessary to formulate a reasonable response. If the hypothetical question appears to be too complex for you to answer, indicate that is the case.
- *Listen to objections.* At times your attorney may object to a question for a variety of reasons. Then you will be asked to answer the question if you can. Listen to the objection. If it involves the syntax of the question, ask for a restatement or simplification. Rarely, your attorney will direct you not to answer the question, but if so, keep quict. At this point, the attorneys may engage in heated colloquy concerning your right to refuse to answer. If that occurs, you should not interfere, but wait until you are given a final instruction whether to answer or not.

Ending the Deposition

At the deposition, you will be asked whether you wish to review the transcript in order to correct any possible errors. This is an important question because it determines whether you waive or reserve the right of signature. A waived signature means the transcript will stand as written by the court reporter as the official record of the deposition. A reserved signature, on the other hand, means that you will have time to review and make any changes in either form or substance, provided you give the reasons for making them. These changes are then added to the deposition by the court reporter, and that becomes the official record of the deposition. Ask for the right to sign the deposition unless otherwise advised by your attorney. Court reporters are not perfect and can make serious mistakes in transcribing your verbal answers. Do a careful review of your transcript and correct any errors.

5

Preparing for Trial

Discourage litigation. Persuade your neighbors to compromise whenever you can. As a peacemaker, the lawyer has superior opportunity of being a good man.

There will still be business enough.

—Abraham Lincoln

The time before trial is crucial. Everyone needs to understand their roles and what is going to happen in the courtroom. As an expert witness, you need time to reflect and synthesize your opinions and their bases.

Depending on the court, your case may be placed on the docket (calendar) anywhere from three months to one year in advance of the trial date. The judge's docket will have a number of potential trials set for the same time in some priority order. Delays are common for a variety of reasons. Perhaps more witnesses need to be deposed, or settlement negotiations are close to resolution. Some judges are sympathetic to the need for continuances. Others hold tight to scheduled deadlines to keep their dockets moving. Either way, you must prepare for trial even before you know the exact trial date.

Developing the Trial Theme

A plausible and convincing trial theme is an important factor in winning a case. The theme provides the jury with a framework to decide the case and gives attorneys the skeleton upon which to develop a strategy for winning. Recent well-publicized cases provide good examples of how a running theme throughout trial can influence the outcome of the case. For example, in the notorious O. J. Simpson trial, the defense portrayed the case as one involving racist police officers who set out to frame Simpson. The prosecution, on the other hand, focused on Simpson's reputation as an abusive and menacing husband, and on physical evidence

Another example of the power of a theme is found in the nationwide tobacco litigation. The plaintiffs characterize the tobacco companies as sinister and knowing purveyors of addictive drugs. On the other hand, the defendant tobacco companies focus on the right of individuals to freely choose whether to purchase and smoke cigarettes. In both of these examples, attorneys for each party use the themes as a filter for the evidence presented to the jury. A good expert witness can help develop these themes by working together with the attorneys.

Preparing the Lawyers

If you have a good rapport with your attorney, you can actively participate in the trial preparation process. One way to accomplish this is to develop a complete list of questions that you want to be asked on direct examination. Interspersed with the questions should be the potential use of various forms of multimedia. Your questions can help the attorney understand the breadth and depth of your opinions so he or she can provide input without missing important aspects of your work.

One of the most effective ways to educate the attorneys you are working with is to go though a mock cross-examination of your opinions before trial. By doing this, not only do they learn the strengths and weaknesses of your opinions, but the process also prepares you for the rigors of cross-examination. Expressing your opinions to someone unfamiliar with the case, such as a new lead attorney, is good practice for testifying in front of the judge and jury. Furthermore, unforeseen and significant questions may very well arise from a fresh perspective and can be helpful in developing new lines of questioning, more focused responses, and different exhibits. Request a mock cross-examination if it is not offered in advance. During the mock cross-examination, the attorney should attempt to push you to the boundaries of your comfort zone. Establish your boundaries and do not cross them. This exercise will instill confidence in you and ensure that you are prepared.

Changing Your Opinion

After the deposition, you and the attorneys should review what went well at the deposition and what did not. The sooner after the deposition, the better, so that the details are still fresh in everyone's mind. This review may very well result in the need for further investigation or analysis. It may also result in new information or data to be considered. Write it down. Develop a checklist for the actions that need to be accomplished before the trial date.

You may change your opinion after the discovery cutoff date if new and important information becomes available. If it is a minor refinement, you can simply make the change and then prepare to justify it in court. If you make a major modification in your opinion, however, you may be deposed on that issue. A change of opinion after the discovery cutoff should be made only if absolutely necessary.

The pretrial period is often very busy, so organization is important. Depending on the nature of the case, you may be asked to accomplish additional tasks prior to the trial based upon your experience, qualifications or capabilities. These tasks may include reviewing other expert testimony or new items uncovered during the discovery process. You may be asked to help develop the trial strategy or pretrial motions. Whatever the task, stay in touch with the attorneys, and make sure they know how and how much you can assist them.[1]

Trial Exhibits

Exhibit preparation is an undervalued aspect of trial preparation. Experts often feel that all they have to do is copy graphs, charts, and pictures from their expert reports and have them blown up for trial exhibits. When they do this, they can present the technical talk to the jurors and show how smart they were in arriving at their opinions. This approach risks losing the attention of the judge and jurors, who will not be moved by a presentation based solely on technical tools.

We live in the age of visual sensation. Large segments of the population play video games, use computers, watch enormous amounts of television, and go to the movies. They less frequently read books, fix their own cars, or

[1] Marc A. Rabinoff and Stephen P. Holmes, *The forensic expert's guide to litigation: The anatomy of a lawsuit* (Horsham, PA: LRP Publications, 1996).

engage in intellectual pursuits in their spare time. These people make up the bulk of jurors. In addition, jury members rarely have any technical training. It takes jurors about two to five minutes to tune out highly technical and, to them, incomprehensible explanations of the expert opinion. Your testimony should be readily understandable by an 18-year-old or an 80-year-old. You need to capture the jury's attention and make an impression that stays with them long after you have left the witness stand.

You capture the minds of jury members through the skillful use of multimedia. Think about the mental paradigm of left brain and right brain. The left side is the rational, logical thought processor. The right side is the creative, imaginative, picture processor. You need to feed both sides of the brain by interspersing logical, rational, linear words and calculations with pictures, animation, and cartoons in a balanced presentation.

Remember the old adage, "a picture is worth a thousand words." Here are seven highly effective ways to visually present information:

1. *Flip Charts.* Flip charts are powerful because the information is produced in front of the jury in real time. It is a form of "chalk talk." Drawings, words, and numbers that are on paper for the jury to see reinforce the words you utter. You need to practice in advance and have the talent to draw and write legibly.
2. *Photographs.* Photographs help the jurors see what you are talking about. You must take care that the photo has sufficient resolution and looks professional. Photos can be displayed via computer or overhead projectors or, if the judge allows, given to each juror individually. Poor photographs can be computer-enhanced if the alterations do not change the basic nature of the information.
3. *Drawings/Computer Graphics.* Nothing sticks in jurors' minds as much as strong visualization. Well-thought-out graphics can allow you to break down complex processes into simple, understandable elements.
4. *Highlighted Critical Documents.* Media professionals can take an important document and highlight a phrase or a portion by dulling the remainder of the page and showing a magnifying glass (or some other technique) to expand what you want the jury to see. This approach should be commingled with other multimedia to relate evidence to your opinions in a visual way.
5. *Models.* Scale models can be costly but are potentially worth every penny. Always consider how your opinions can be enhanced if you have a scale model available. Make sure that sufficient fidelity to reality is maintained, or the other side may object and the judge may agree, in which case your model will not be allowed in the courtroom. Also,

remember that the other side can use your model to demonstrate its own points.

6. *Video.* Video is good because it is what jurors are used to watching. A good narration by you is absolutely necessary to accompany the images shown. Be wary of blurry, fast motion and poorly lit or distant footage. The video needs to be precise and short. Any video longer than three to five minutes loses its force.
7. *Animation.* Animation is the frontier in multimedia for the courtroom. It is used extensively to reconstruct what happened and why. A 90-second animation can be the show-and-tell that makes the difference in a case. On the computer, a simulation can be looked at from any viewpoint and manipulated to run at any speed, including slowing or stopping motion. Not all courts allow animation, for fear that it may unduly prejudice the jury. Your job as an expert will be to make sure the animation accurately depicts your opinions and cannot be used effectively by the other side to illustrate their points.

Your use of multimedia tools does not necessarily have to be overly expensive or technologically sophisticated. The most important thing is that presentation be engaging and interesting. The combination of multimedia with your testimony can be compelling if you diligently prepare a powerful storyline that drives your opinions deep into the minds of the judge and jurors.

Motions

Following the pleadings and the discovery phase of the case, the lawyers representing each side in the litigation may file a variety of motions either to avoid trial or to narrow the scope of issues to be tried. Some motions seek the exclusion of evidence or testimony, including an expert's opinion (the *Daubert* motion). Others, such as a motion for summary judgment, ask the court to dismiss the case on legal grounds when the material facts are not in dispute. The use of motions can be an efficient and cost-effective way to determine the relative strength of the opposing positions.

Pursuant to Rule 56 of the Federal Rules of Civil Procedure, in a *motion for summary judgment* a party argues that there is no genuine issue of material fact and that the moving party is entitled to a judgment as a matter of law. Typically, a motion for summary judgment does not require a hearing. Instead, the parties submit documents, deposition transcripts, and affidavits to show that none of the central facts of the case is in dispute. If a plaintiff's case hinges not on facts, but on the opinion of an expert on issues such as standard of care or causation, it is likely the defendant's attorney will move to exclude the expert's testimony under *Daubert* and then seek summary judgment to dismiss the case. Without a factual dispute, there is no reason for the case to be heard by the jury. Thus, the judge can decide the case based on the law. "In many cases, a court can resolve *Daubert* issues when addressing a motion for summary judgment. If the court ultimately determines that expert testimony is inadmissible and the party has no other evidence to support its cause of action, summary judgment is generally granted. Although either party can file a summary judgment motion challenging the other party's expert witness, most of these motions are brought by defendants challenging plaintiff's experts."[2]

If a case is not dismissed, the opposing party may still ask the court to preclude or limit the expert testimony in a motion *in limine*. A motion *in limine* is a motion to prevent an opposing party from introducing or mentioning in front of a jury a particular fact.[3] In federal cases, such motions are governed by Federal Rules of Evidence Rule 104(a), which states that a party may petition the court to preclude questions, facts, or evidence that are so prejudicial that merely asking of the question or presenting the facts or evidence will have a prejudicial and/or inflammatory effect on the jury, despite an objection that could be raised. An example of a topic or issue that falls within these boundaries is insurance. Often, litigation involves insurance companies that may be forced to pay damages. If juries learn that a party has insurance coverage, they may refrain from awarding damages to that party. Referral to insurance in and of itself can be grounds enough for a mistrial in certain cases. In other cases where the mere mention of insurance does not cause a problem, intentional or continued reference to insurance in testimony can bring the trial to a halt.[4]

"Motions *in limine* have become more common in civil litigation since *Daubert*."[5] At an *in limine* hearing, one party asks the court to limit or bar altogether the testimony of an expert for the opposing party on the basis that the expert does not meet the *Daubert* criteria, contending that the expert lacks the necessary knowledge, skill, experience, training, or education to render opinions that will assist the jury in reaching a just decision. A successful motion *in limine* can cause havoc in a case if a judge rules that the expert's opinion may not be introduced in the trial. As mentioned above, if the expert opinion is the lynchpin of a party's case, exclusion of the expert most likely will result in the case being dismissed as a matter of law. As an

[2] Eric Pierson, *1999 Witley expert witness update: New developments in personal injury litigation* (New York: Aspen Law and Business, 1998), 129.
[3] Rabinoff and Holmes.
[4] Rabinoff and Holmes.
[5] Eric Pierson, *1999 Witley expert witness update: New developments in personal injury litigation* (New York: Aspen Law and Business, 1998), 129.

expert, you must consider the likelihood that the opposing party will file a motion *in limine*. Likewise, you should be prepared to assist your attorney either in responding to motions or in filing motions to exclude the introduction of evidence by the other side. Reviews should be requested of any demonstrative evidence, such as charts or diagrams that the opposing expert intends to use, so that you have an opportunity to request exclusion of any prejudicial material before it is shown to the jury. Even though preliminary motions need not always be submitted in writing, doing so may increase the chance of success, especially if the authorities and grounds for the motion are clearly referenced and articulated. Potential objections to such motions should also be anticipated and counterarguments prepared.[6]

Motions regarding the admissibility of expert testimony can be made at any stage of trial proceedings. The opposing side's expert testimony can be attacked at deposition, in a motion *in limine*, in a motion for summary judgment, at a separate *Daubert* hearing, at trial, or in a motion for directed verdict. Motions on the admissibility of expert testimony are often crucial to the outcome of a case and will be expediently filed whenever questionable expert testimony is encountered.

Understanding the Judge

Know and understand the judge. Especially in light of *Daubert* and related cases, the judge is responsible for determining the reliability and the relevance of expert testimony and other evidence. In executing this charge, the judge will determine just how broad — or narrow — testimony can be. Judges have two different approaches in this regard. Some will allow everything, whether or not it is directly material, on the theory that this will be fair to both sides and in the hope that the jury will determine the relevance. Others will restrict what is admissible and will narrow the focus in order to expedite the trial. Both approaches can be effective, but it is important to understand which will be employed and to tailor testimony accordingly.

It is also helpful to think of the judge as part of the jury. If effective and convincing, your testimony will have an impact on the judge. At times, the judge may ask questions, and at the end of the trial it is the judge who delivers the jury instructions, based on the evidence and opinions presented at trial. The jury will then decide the case based on those instructions. A judge who understands the case may be more effective in transmitting clear instructions, which typically leads to a more just outcome.

[6] Robert C. Clifford, *Qualifying and attacking expert witnesses* (Santa Ana, CA: James Publishing Group, 1990).

Types of Juries

A jury is a group of people who are summoned and sworn by the court in order to decide on the facts in issue at a trial. There are two types of juries in the American judicial system: the grand jury and the petit jury. There are two types of grand juries — the regular grand jury and the special grand jury. Each performs a distinct but equally important function. A regular grand jury considers bills of indictment, hears witnesses, and determines whether there is sufficient probable cause to believe that an accused person should stand trial. A grand jury usually consists of fifteen to twenty-three members who serve a term of duty ranging from six to eighteen months which can be extended by up to ninety days should the grand jury not complete its charge within an allotted term. A special grand jury is comprised of seven to eleven citizens of a city or county charged by a court to investigate and report upon any condition which tends to promote criminal activity in the community. A grand jury is not obligated to hear both sides of a case, nor does it determine guilt or innocence.

Expert witnesses are more commonly involved with cases heard by petit jurors. Petit jurors are summoned to serve for civil and criminal jury trials. In federal civil cases, the size of the jury can range from six to twelve members. Criminal trials, on the other hand, and most state civil trials, require twelve jurors with a minimum of one alternate. Alternate jurors minimize the potential for retrial should one of the jurors have to leave due to illness, personal emergency, or other valid reason.

Jury Selection

The trial process starts with the selection of a jury. Trial by a jury of peers is a fundamental right of every American citizen, guaranteed by the Seventh Amendment to the Constitution of the United States. In addition to this right, jury duty is an important responsibility of being an American citizen which can be required once every two years or more.

Jury duty is mandatory. Potential jurors are randomly selected from a variety of sources. Some jurisdictions use voter registration records; others use sources such as customer mailing lists, telephone directories, and utility company lists. California law allows courts to use the names of all persons who have driver's licenses or identification cards issued by the Department of Motor Vehicles. To be eligible to serve as a juror, a person must be a citizen of the United States, understand English, be at least eighteen years of age, and be physically and mentally capable of serving. Additionally, some jurisdictions stipulate that a potential juror must never have been convicted of a felony. Potential jurors are mailed a qualification questionnaire that is completed, returned, and evaluated by the court. Potential jurors who meet all of the qualifications to serve are requested to appear at the designated court through a formal summons.

Many potential jurors are reluctant to serve for a variety of reasons. This is especially true if the trial to which they are assigned promises to be long and complex. Individuals must serve unless they have a valid and compelling reason to be excused, such as young children to care for or a prohibitive medical condition. All juries are selected on the first day the prospective jurors report to the court for duty. In most jurisdictions, if a prospective juror is not selected that day, his or her jury service is over. If selected, however, jurors serve for the duration of the case to which they are assigned.

Prospective jurors report to court, where they are questioned by the judge and attorneys. Initially, the judge introduces the nature of the case to be tried, the names of the opposing parties involved in the case, and the attorneys who will be representing them. The judge asks each prospective juror basic facts concerning marital status, occupation, and previous jury involvement, if any. This information helps to ease the prospective jurors into their potential roles while also introducing them to the judge and opposing attorneys. After these introductions are completed, the business of jury selection begins.

Voir dire is the process used to examine prospective jurors under oath regarding their qualifications and suitability to serve in that specific trial. The purpose of *voir dire* is to eliminate potential jurors who may be biased and therefore unable to make a fair and impartial decision based on the evidence presented. During this process, the judge and attorneys question the prospective jurors to determine whether any juror has prior knowledge or information about the case, the parties involved in the case, the litigating attorneys, or the experts or other witnesses. Additionally, the questioning is intended to determine if a juror harbors any opinions that may affect his or her ability to be both fair and impartial. In state courts, attorneys can question jurors during *voir dire* and can question each potential juror as to their work, family, religion, union membership, or other such topic in order to ascertain potential bias. In federal courts, the judge alone can question and select the jurors, although the judge can entertain questions suggested by attorneys from either side. In some cases, judges will examine prospective jurors individually and apart from other prospective jurors in order to fairly evaluate a person who is hesitant to speak in front of others.

The jury selection process also provides the opportunity for each side to challenge potential jurors or ask for them to be excluded from participating in the trial. There are two types of challenges — the challenge for cause and the peremptory challenge. Challenges for cause are unlimited in number and require that the attorney show potential bias on the part of the juror which renders that person incapable of reaching a fair and impartial verdict. Peremptory challenges, on the other hand, are limited in number, and do not require that the reason be stated or substantiated. An attorney may use a peremptory challenge based on feeling, hunch, or intuition to exclude potential jurors felt to be unsympathetic to their side. The attorneys should "look for jurors who may 'match' the important expert witness. It is most advantageous if a similar, or at least a complementary, type of juror judges your expert at trial."[7] Peremptory challenges provide the attorneys from both sides some choice in the make-up of the jury. Both sides have the same number of challenges. Potential jurors who are challenged will be struck, or excused, from service in the case. The actual jury and alternates are then chosen from the remaining, unchallenged prospective jurors.

The challenge process is not meant to offend prospective jurors. To the contrary, the system of challenges helps strengthen the jury system. "Plaintiffs will excuse jurors perceived to be pro-defendant. Defendants will dismiss jurors believed to be pro-plaintiff. Through this method of selection and challenge, greater confidence is instilled that the jury system is neutral, fair, and unbiased."[8]

Jury selection is of such significance that statistical analysis and survey techniques are sometimes employed in assisting the trial team in identifying pro-plaintiff and pro-defense jurors. In a commonly used process, 300 to 500 community residents are asked first to listen to a summary of the case and then to render a verdict. The verdicts are then correlated with the demographic and attitudinal information concerning the respondents in order to develop a statistical profile of pro-plaintiff and pro-defense jurors. Additionally, these profiles can be used to establish the potential worst- and best-case outcomes for the case which can serve as an extremely powerful tool for use in settlement or at trial.[9]

"When a jury has been accepted by both sides, the jury members are sworn to try the case. Each juror must set aside personal beliefs and emotions, and decide the case solely from the evidence that is presented, the reasonable inferences from the evidence and pursuant to the instructions of the court."[10]

Trial preparation is the time when you develop your opinions for delivery. It is the time to practice and perfect the presentation. For both attorneys and experts, it is a frenetic time. Pretrial motions such as *Daubert* challenges must be handled, fact witnesses must be lined up and prepared, the trial theme

[7] Faust F. Rossi, *Expert witnesses* (Chicago, IL: American Bar Association, 1991), 291.
[8] Richard Alexander, Jury duty in California: An overview of jury trials, *Consumer Law Page* (April 2001), 6, www.consumerlawpage.com.
[9] Joseph A. Rice, Twelve angry men? Think again, *Jury Research Institute*, www.jri-inc.com.
[10] The Fayette Circuit Court, Information for Jurors: Juror handbook, 5, www.aoc.state.ky.us/fayettecourts.

and strategies must be established, and individuals from all facets of the case must come together as a team.

Trials are real-life dramas that challenge your creativity and test your resolve. Cases change continually and sometimes dramatically as new information is uncovered and opposing strategies unfold. Be flexible. Do not be surprised if you are reordering your testimony the night before you take the stand. Work as a team with your attorney, and provide all the assistance your expertise allows.

6

The Courtroom Drama

We have a criminal jury system which is superior to any in the world; and its efficiency is only marred by the difficulty of finding twelve men every day who don't know anything and can't read.

—Mark Twain

The Jury — The True "Audience" of the Trial

"A jury is a group of people who are summoned and sworn in order to decide on the facts in issue at a trial."[1] The judge decides all issues of law, but the jurors are the ultimate arbiters of the facts that are presented. Their judgment is, in large part, influenced by the credibility of the testimony they hear. "Jurors don't vote on any clear sense of absolute truth. They vote on their impressions."[2]

To decide the case, the jury deliberates on the evidence presented and delivers a verdict to the judge. For the expert witness, the jury is the key constituency when trial testimony is being offered. Answers to questions must

[1] Marc A. Rabinoff and Stephen P. Holmes, *The forensic expert's guide to litigation: The anatomy of a lawsuit* (Horsham, PA: LRP Publications, 1996), 42.
[2] Anne L. Finger , How to be your own best expert witness, *Medical Economics* (March 22, 1999), 96–100.

be directed to and have an impact on the jury. To have an impact, the jury must understand what is being said. It is more important for the jury to hear what it needs to know rather than to hear everything that the expert knows. Exhibits and demonstrative aids should be used and explained in a clear, attractive, and understandable way, but should not require lengthy explanation. The jury will reward and find favor in the side that helps them clearly understand the technical aspects of the case.[3]

From the moment the jurors are sworn in, they are the real focus. Which jurors are paying attention, taking notes, shaking their heads? Which ones feel what bonds? Which juror looks like a leader, and who may become the jury foreman? "Each aspect of the trial — *voir dire*, the opening statement, the presentation of evidence, the cross-examination of the opposing witnesses, and the closing summation — is directed to convincing the jury to adopt your version of the facts and to return a favorable verdict."[4]

Opening Statements

The trial begins with the presentation of the opening statement. "To many legal experts this is the second opportunity in the court trial process to win or lose a case," after jury selection.[5] Attorneys for the plaintiff, in a civil case, or for the prosecution, in a criminal case, usually are the first tell the jury what they believe the evidence will prove. Plaintiffs or prosecutors typically occupy the counsel table closest to the jury and present their opening statement first because they have the burden of proof. The defendant's attorney will then make an opening statement; however, in some cases, the defense attorney has the option of delaying this opening statement until after the plaintiffs have completed presenting their case.

The opening statements reveal to the judge and jury the opposing story lines. In the opening statement, the lawyer outlines for the jury the issues involved in the case and the evidence to be presented that will firmly establish the validity of the claim or the defense. It is also an opportune time to introduce and explain in general terms any expert testimony to be used in the case. The lawyer should explain to the jury the evidence to be presented, show how it will be presented, provide a brief overview of the qualifications of the expert(s) who will be testifying, and describe in broad terms the basis for the expert opinions. Exhibits can be used to better illustrate points made during the opening statement and can be far more effective and convincing

[3] Faust F. Rossi, *Expert witnesses* (Chicago: American Bar Association, 1991).
[4] Robert C. Clifford, *Qualifying and attacking expert witnesses* (Santa Ana, CA: James Publishing Group, 1990), 350.
[5] Rabinoff and Homes, 30.

than oratory alone. The opening statement also provides an opportunity to address any potential weaknesses in expert testimony to be offered. By introducing such weaknesses during the opening statement, the lawyer has an opportunity to preempt the opposing side's argument concerning that testimony, while building credibility with the jury.[6]

The opening statement is an opportunity to educate the jury on the process of the trial. The lawyer will explain why expert witnesses are being used and why they were selected. This explanation increases the legitimacy of both the expert and the expert's role in the case. An opening statement is effective if it increases the jury's interest in the testimony and evidence to be presented and if it piques curiosity in what the experts will say. The opening statement should also prepare the jury for the more antagonistic aspects of the trial, such as an aggressive cross-examination, so that they are not surprised, and also so that they do not see the lawyer, or the party being represented, in bad light. Juries often appreciate candor and, as a result, more readily understand the lawyer's approach. [7]

Opening statements are not considered to be evidence and are, in theory, intended simply to acquaint the jurors with the nature of the case. In reality, however, the importance of the opening statement cannot be overstated. The opening statement is the first opportunity for the lawyers representing the opposing sides to explain the basis for their cases and to establish the theme for the trial. The opening statement sets the tone for the trial. Fortunately or not, this first impression often profoundly influences the final verdict. Surveys conducted during and after trials indicate that a juror's initial impression of a case based upon the opening statements often reflects his or her ultimate verdict.[8] Your duty as an expert is to consult with your attorncy in the preparation of the opening statement to make sure the attorney accurately represents your credentials and opinions.

Direct Examination

Direct examination is the heart of the case. It consists of questions posted to a lay or expert witness to elicit facts that corroborate a party's theory of the case. Direct examination is also the best opportunity to present the facts and reinforce the theme that will convince the jury and win the case. Unlike in depositions, where experts are advised to be brief and responsive, at trial experts have the opportunity to expand their answers. The goal of direct

[6] Clifford.
[7] Rossi.
[8] Clifford.

examination is to educate the judge and jury; therefore, it is imperative that direct testimony be understandable, interesting, and persuasive.

Effective direct examination must tell the entire story in a logical, cogent, and memorable way. Good direct examination should boil down all of the information and research to the essential elements, including any expert opinions. Direct testimony should not only hit the high points and refute any weak points of the case. It should also identify any weaknesses so that on cross-examination the jury has already heard the issue and is impressed by the candor of the witness in revealing facts that may be brought up by the other side. This may also include the expert's compensation and the number of times an expert has testified as an expert witness.

It is important to remember that jurors may have relatively limited attention spans. The members of the jury will be making a great effort to listen to, understand, and remember the testimony in the case but can become fatigued by information overload. Visual exhibits should be used whenever possible to illustrate key points, and common phrases and terms should be used repeatedly throughout the trial to emphasize the important points and images you wish to convey to the jury. It is wise, therefore, to limit direct expert testimony to hours, not days. Such a time limit requires discipline, organization, practice, and a great deal of preparation on the part of both the expert and the attorney. A time limit should also improve the quality of the witness's' testimony by making it more succinct.

On the day you are scheduled to testify, you should be at the court well in advance of the time you are scheduled to be on the witness stand. It is important to understand that the scheduled time to testify may, and more often than not will, change. Judges often change timetables without prior notice. You should be prepared to wait until it is time to testify.

The first fifteen minutes of your presentation should include the most important information and should get to the "bottom line."[9] In this period, the quality of both you as an expert and your expert opinions need to be established. It is critical that your qualifications be established prior to providing any opinions. Once the qualifications are established, you should explain the issues of the case, present your opinions concerning those issues, and provide the basis for those opinions. Certainly, this is a lot to accomplish in fifteen minutes, but if accomplished, the jury will most likely understand and, more importantly, remember your expert testimony. The balance of the time for direct testimony should be used to answer questions that serve to further educate, clarify, and reinforce the opinions provided in the first fifteen minutes of the testimony.

[9] Eric Pierson, *1999 Witley expert update: New developments in personal injury litigation* (New York: Aspen Law and Business, 1998).

Direct examination can be disrupted by the opposing lawyers if they conduct a *voir dire* to inquire into your qualifications as an expert. As with jury selection, the *voir dire* is an examination of an expert's qualifications, but is more often a preliminary mini cross-examination.[10] "The expert here needs to turn her attention from persuading a lawyer and the opposing client to teaching the jury in a way that will make the testimony understandable and consistent with the jury's common sense."[11] The suggestions provided in Chapter 4 for answering questions in a deposition are also applicable in the trial setting — don't lose your temper, speak clearly, finish your answers, correct your answers if need be, read fine print in documents, listen to objections, try to avoid possible hypothetical questions, be consistent, etc.

Direct examination is often a test of the credibility and preparation of the expert witness; therefore, your credibility as an expert witness must be consciously maintained. Many times, an expert's credibility is damaged during direct examination due to the nature of questioning by the expert's own lawyer. How does this happen? The jury knows that the lawyer is hired to be an advocate for one side, yet the witness is supposed to be neutral. If the witness looks like a "hired gun," his or her testimony suffers. It is a paradoxical situation. On one hand, the expert will present opinions that reflect the viewpoints of the party that hired him or her; on the other hand, the expert must show independence of thought and no bias in coming up with those opinions.

You must be perceived as a responsible, objective observer. This is especially important in light of the role of the expert witness. Whereas fact witnesses can only testify to facts of which they have personal knowledge, expert witnesses testify to probabilities and assumptions. You can also testify to hearsay, if it is the kind of information that would normally be relied upon in your business.[12] You are entitled — and expected — to give opinions. The fact witness, generally, may not.

Remember that anything you say in open court or in deposition is public record. Your statements may stay with you for the rest of your career. That stretched statement you made five years ago can be thrown back in your face at any time, to your regret. Your honor and credibility is all you have to offer. You must protect them from even the hint of tarnish.

[10] Steven Lubet, *Expert testimony: A guide for expert witnesses and the lawyers who examine them* (Boston: National Institute For Trial Advocacy, 1998).
[11] David M. Malone and Paul J. Zwier, *Effective expert testimony* (Notre Dame, IN: National Institute for Trial Advocacy, 2000), 88.
[12] Knox D. Nunnally, Use of experts (State Bar of Texas Professional Development Advanced Personal Injury Law Course, 1987).

The Role of the Attorney

In many cases, the success or failure of the case depends on the effectiveness of the expert during the trial. The examining attorney should bear in mind the primary objectives of educating and ultimately persuading the jury when organizing the direct testimony of experts. Additionally, the attorney can enhance the effectiveness of the expert by carefully orchestrating the way expert testimony is presented. This can be achieved by organizing the direct testimony of experts using a method that includes an "introduction, tickler, qualifications, tender, opinions, bases for opinions, rationale, and anticipated cross-examination" challenges and questions.[13]

Experts should be introduced in a way that establishes a rapport between them and the jury and that reinforces that they are real people and not simply educated or famous mercenaries. As an expert, you need to be informed about what other experts have said in the case, but you should not be heavily involved in the proceedings. The directing attorney must ensure that you look and act in a way that reinforces your role as an independent professional, rather than allowing you to be perceived as a co-counsel. Additionally, it is important that you avoid the appearance or perception of being a professional witness, which might alienate certain jurors. The opinion of any expert is greatly diminished if the jury believes that the opinion has been purchased.

The examining attorney relies as much on the credibility of an expert as on the opinions that expert provides in support of the case. Consequently, attorneys should present your qualifications and establish your expertise as early and convincingly as possible. Copies of your *curriculum vitae* can be marked as an exhibit, introduced into evidence, and provided to the jury. This method saves time by obviating the need to go through this information in oral testimony. Still, the attorney should clearly convey the relevance of your specific qualifications as they relate to the case, as well as your ability to apply these qualifications to the actual issues involved in the case. In some jurisdictions, the formal presentation of an expert and qualifications is referred to as a "tender." The act of tender provides the opportunity for the opposing attorneys to either perform a *voir dire* inquiry or, if allowed by the judge, to present a *Daubert* challenge based on an objection to the claim of expertise.[14]

The examination of an expert can be accomplished through either of two methods: the question-and-answer technique or the narrative-testimony technique. In the question-and-answer technique, the attorney first asks you

[13] D.M. Malone and P.J. Zwier, *Effective expert testimony* (Notre Dame, IN: National Institute for Trial Advocacy, 2000).

[14] S. Lubet, *Expert testimony: A guide for expert witnesses and the lawyers who examine them* (Boston: National Institute of Trial Advocacy, 1998).

if you have an opinion, and then asks you to present your opinion and the basis on which it was formulated. The question-and-answer technique, which is also referred to as the "two-step" or "opinion first" technique, gives the attorney more control over the testimony. The attorney can, through you, emphasize the most important points of the testimony and show that your opinion is well-reasoned and thoughtful.[15] Care must be taken in using this technique, however, because Rule 611 of the Federal Rules of Evidence states that attorneys cannot ask questions that suggest or contain the answer during direct examination. "The two-step approach seems to be favored by judges but it draws out the process, focuses the jury's attention on the experts, creates a sense of anticipation and the impression that something important is happening."[16]

Unlike the question-and-answer technique, the narrative technique provides a forum for you to offer your opinions and the bases for them in a single, albeit sometimes lengthy, answer. In this technique, the directing attorney should provide an exhibit such as a chart, diagram, or outline of events that helps frame the narrative and captures the key points to be addressed. While the narrative technique can be hard to follow and digest, it allows you to appear more genuine to the jury and is especially effective where you have a gregarious and engaging personality.[17]

The attorney conducting the direct examination has a number of responsibilities in preparing you for testifying. It is the responsibility of the attorney to prepare you for *voir dire* questions and/or *Daubert* challenges. The attorney must ensure that each witness has reviewed all of the applicable evidence, depositions, and records, as well as the questions to be asked and the exhibits to be used during the direct examination. It is critical that you review your own prior deposition testimony so that your direct testimony and the deposition do not conflict. Additionally, familiarity with the deposition testimony helps you avoid impeachment by your own deposition on cross-examination. You must be prepared to admit and explain any changes in your opinion subsequent to the deposition.[18]

Of course, the preparation process can be a two-way street. Remember that the primary objective of the attorney conducting direct examination is to introduce evidence, opinions, and conclusions that reinforce the theme and edify the case. As an expert, you can help by providing a complete list of suggested questions to be used for direct examination and the order and location of trial exhibits that accompany your testimony. Additionally, you

[15] Mark A. Dombroff, Prepare and present your expert witness, *For The Defense* (August 1984).
[16] Rossi, 219.
[17] Dombroff.
[18] K.D. Nunnally, Use of Experts, State Bar of Texas Professional Development Advanced Personal Injury Law Course, 2.

should work with the attorney to ensure that your testimony is succinct, interesting and easy for the jury to understand. This can be accomplished by spending time with the attorney, talking, exchanging information and ideas, and challenging each other regarding the strategy and presentation of the proposed testimony. It is also a good idea to rehearse and critique the direct examination on videotape so that it can be perfected prior to delivery.

Meet with the attorney just before your scheduled testimony to make sure you are ready, to make any last-minute changes in strategy if needed, and to finalize the schedule, logistics, and contingency plans. If you have not been present during the trial, this meeting provides the opportunity to be brought up to date on what has transpired in the trial, including insight into the style and strategies of the judge and opposing attorneys. You can also gain insight into the best ways to present your testimony by reviewing the names, backgrounds, occupations, and educational levels of the jury. This insight will help you focus on the jury and use analogies and examples that are appropriate to jurors' backgrounds. Make sure you talk *to* the members of the jury, not down to them. Simplify your testimony so that it can be understood by the lay persons present, including the judge, jury, attorneys from both sides, and most of the other witnesses who will testify.

Building the Case

The attorney is responsible for convincing the jury to accept and believe his or her theory of the case. To accomplish this, the jury must accept and believe the attorney's trial theme and experts over the opposing side's theme and experts. Concise and clear direct testimonies are one way to convince the jury. Terminology and phrases that lead the jury to the desired conclusion should be used consistently throughout direct examination.

The use of high-impact visual materials is strongly suggested during direct examination. Major opinions and supporting facts that are visually displayed are essential in building the case. On a single or simple series of charts or graphs using different color codes and graphics, multiple opinions and their bases can be clearly communicated and effectively differentiated. You should also be ready to comment on the theories presented in the opposing side's expert testimonies. This process, commonly known as "theory differentiation," is intended to expose the flaws and failures of the other experts' theories without attacking the experts themselves.[19]

You should also understand the value of letting the jury know you as an individual, not just as an authority. Personalizing your testimony is in many ways more important than the testimony itself in establishing your credibility.

[19] Lubet.

Use plain language to explain any technical subject matter in terms the jury can fully understand. Use examples, metaphors, and analogies the jury can relate to from real-life situations in support of your explanation of the more complex points and opinions in your testimony. These tools should be prepared and practiced in advance but should appear spontaneous to the jury.[20]

Your direct examination should clearly articulate your opinion and illustrate how you arrived at it, why that particular opinion is relevant, and where you are going next with your testimony. Your attorney must help you create a bond of trust with the jury that allows you to persuasively build the case.[21]

Preparing for Cross-Examination

When the attorney has completed the direct examination, the opposing attorney has the opportunity to cross-examine the witness. "Successful cross-examination begins with thorough preparation and pre-trial discovery before the witness testifies."[22]

Attorneys should obtain information regarding any and all opposing witnesses, but this is especially important for opposing experts. The information to be gathered includes the identities, qualifications, proffered opinions, foundational bases and data for those opinions, publications, previous testimonies provided, and fees.[23] Within these areas lie the bases to challenge the credibility of an expert or to diminish the impact of the expert's testimony. Additionally, the lead attorney should be conversant in each expert's area of expertise as it pertains to the case. This allows the attorney to properly prepare for conducting cross-examination. By knowing the expert witness's strengths and weaknesses, the strategy to be used on cross-examination can and should be planned out well in advance. It is also a good idea to plan and practice alternative approaches in the event that the primary cross-examination strategy is unsuccessful.[24]

As an expert, it is important that you understand the lawyer's perspective and preparation for cross-examination. Just as you can help the attorney representing your side of the case, the experts for the opposing side help the opposing attorneys prepare. You should carefully review your deposition to prepare for questions by the opposing counsel and have appropriate responses planned. Expect a challenge by the opposing counsel to your assumptions or methodology, and anticipate the questions that will come if

[20] Lubet.
[21] Malone and Zwier.
[22] Nunnally, 46.
[23] Roger Haydock and John Sonsteng, *Advocacy: Examining witnesses: Direct, cross and expert witnessing* (Eagan, MN: West Publishing, 1994).
[24] Nunnally.

you have a weakness that is uncovered. Be prepared for the possibility of having your expert report introduced as evidence by the opposing attorney when an inconsistency or discrepancy exists between the testimony and the expert report. Examining your own testimony as if it were the testimony of an opposing expert is an excellent way of preparing for cross-examination.

It is also wise to familiarize yourself with the traps that lawyers use in cross-examination. Attorneys may try to use their opponents' experts to qualify and add credibility to their own. This can be accomplished through questioning aimed at steering an opposing expert to recognize — under oath — the expertise and reputation of their own experts in their given fields.

Sometimes an attorney will intentionally omit one or two key elements during direct examination in hopes that the opposing attorney will, on cross-examination, bring out those key elements. Evidence introduced and substantiated on cross-examination often has a greater impact than evidence introduced on direct. Regardless of the tactics or strategies involved, you should prepare as diligently for cross-examination as you did for direct testimony. Being ill-prepared and surprised on cross-examination can destroy your credibility as well as the entire case for your side. Be mentally and physically prepared for a potentially aggressive confrontation by the opposing attorney.

Cross-Examination

"False testimony may be in the eye of the beholder. We have a great system to root out liars. It's called cross-examination. There definitely are expert witnesses who'll say anything for money, but these liars are quickly exposed."[25]

From the perspective of the expert witness, litigation may appear to be an unfair battle fought in alien surroundings. An expert tends to believe in a universal truth or scientific principle that — with the facts — will make the case understandable. The opposing attorney believes that facts are relative, depending on whose eyes are observing, and that the truths become evident as facts are explained in the proper light. Through cross-examination, it is the obligation of the opposing attorney to shift the perception of reality. Your attorney believes in the same principles and will apply them during cross-examination of the opposing expert.

In order to conduct an effective cross-examination, many attorneys follow Irving Youger's Ten Commandments for cross-examining attorneys. These commandments are:

[25] Mark Crane, How do expert witnesses get away with lying? *Medical Economics* (January 11, 1999), 155.

1. Be brief.
2. Ask short questions; use plain words.
3. Ask leading questions.
4. Ask only questions to which you already know the answers.
5. Don't let the witness merely repeat his direct testimony.
6. Don't let the witness explain.
7. Listen to his witness's answer.
8. Don't quarrel with the witness.
9. Avoid the one question too many.
10. Save the argument for summation.[26]

Through the use of these or similar tactics, the opposing attorney will first attempt to impeach you and your testimony. In the context of litigation, impeachment does not merely highlight an error of judgment or fact; rather impeachment discredits the witness as a reliable source — the kiss of death for an expert. Impeachment is normally based on inconsistencies in an expert's testimonies and/or opinions. Such discrepancies can be found between deposition and courtroom testimonies, among unsupported or conflicting reports, or between previously published works and current testimony. Even public statements and presentations can be used if the differences are of sufficient magnitude.[27] An impeached expert is of no value and will be a detriment to the case.

If impeachment is not possible, the opposing attorney will then attempt to diminish the impact of your testimony. "The effectiveness of the expert's testimony depends largely on the logic of his work product, his ability to clearly describe his work and state his opinions, and his readiness to answer challenging questions on cross-examination. Of crucial importance for the expert is to maintain his credibility in front of the jury."[28] Of course, the most effective way to diminish the impact of an expert is to challenge the expert's credibility. One method that has been used is to attack the expert on his or her motives for being involved in the case. The directing attorney wants the jury to see you as an interested and educated third party whose intent is to see that truth prevails. The opposing attorney wants the jury to see you as a mercenary motivated primarily, if not solely, by money, whose testimony, as a result, is tainted or biased. The logic is that if you are highly compensated, the jury is more likely to view you as a mercenary. But this argument has two sides. Today's juries are well aware of the importance of experts and that

[26] Nunnally, 47.
[27] John P. Coniglio, The expert witness: A primer on your activities, *Professional Safety* (January 2002), 34–39.
[28] Michael E. Sacks, *An overview of the law: A guide for testifying and consulting experts* (Horsham, PA: LRP Publications, 1995), 26.

an expert of impeccable qualifications will likely be well-compensated. In reality, some juries are impressed by the level of compensation that an expert receives and may therefore lend more credibility to your testimony on that basis. "Although the jury might be surprised at the high compensation an expert receives, cross-examining an expert about his fee is generally not effective."[29]

The back-and-forth process of direct and cross-examination amounts to high-stakes intellectual chess played in the context of the courtroom. Directing attorneys go to great lengths to establish your credibility as an expert, knowing that, if properly accomplished, the jury will lend you an aura of authority and impartiality and as a result be more inclined to accept your testimony. The job of the cross-examining attorney is to reduce the effect of this direct testimony and to diminish the aura carefully crafted by the opposing side. This is a formidable task.[30]

It is important for you to understand the objective of cross-examination — to persuade the jury by whatever means available to accept the cross-examining attorney's version of the truth. Bearing this in mind, you should remain calm. Maintain your poise. Realize that the opposing attorney is simply doing a job. If the cross-examining attorney goes too far, he or she may be seen as pummeling you, which can, in fact, rally the jury to your side. Focus on doing your job. Always address your responses to the jury. "Jurors are, in effect, the consumers of the 'product,' and their views of the issues in a case often differ dramatically from those of risk managers, attorneys, and experts."[31]

Cross-examination will be the most challenging part of the trial. Be cooperative and educational by supporting and explaining your opinions without becoming defensive. Certainly, cross-examination is a contest — but it is an intellectual contest where the goal is not to defeat the opposing party, but rather to win over the jury. "When your opinion is well-founded and based on sound principles and fact, [cross-examination] presents another opportunity to support that opinion. Questions may also open the door for the expert to interject additional facts and understanding."[32]

Opposing Counsel's Strategies

An expert's interpretation of facts is most often the primary point of contention and an object of focus in cross-examination. Unless the issue is on

[29] Clifford, 433.
[30] Clifford.
[31] Joseph A. Rice, Twelve angry men? Think again, *Jury Research Institute*, 1, www.jri-inc.com.
[32] Coniglio, 11.

the cutting edge of technology, the scientific and technical principles are generally agreed on by both sides. Therefore, it is the duty of the opposing attorney to make you reexamine your understanding of the facts so that they can be interpreted more favorably for the opposing side. This attorney may use the four Cs in cross-examination — commit, credit, confront, and contrast — or one or more of the following techniques as identified by Malone and Zwier:

1. *Constructive Cross-examination*: Initially, the opposing attorney will go over all facts agreed to by both sides. The questions asked are "yes" or "no" questions and are incremental in nature, with seemingly little impact. Thus, you will likely start your cross-examination saying "yes" to most of the questions without amplification. Then the attorney will suddenly shift into the gray areas and skillfully push you into agreeing in areas favorable to his or her side. Psychologically, you are predisposed to continue agreement, having developed a nonthreatening relationship with the "yes" question-answer routine. You will be pushed to your limit with lines of questioning based on your earlier answers. The attorney will go for a series of admissions as the questioning toughens. By skillfully using incremental questions, the cumulative results of the series of questions make the opposing side's point or diminish your testimony.
2. *Micro Cross-examination*: The opposing attorney will confront you with any contradictions and errors in your work and testimony. The attorney and staff have thoroughly researched your professional life. Everything you have written on the subject to which you have previously testified under oath is potential material for cross-examination. You probably have written an expert report and given a deposition. This is especially inviting territory. The attorney will not hesitate to confront you with conflicting testimony from other witnesses who have already testified. This battle is usually conducted on a very high intellectual level where every utterance you make is important.
3. *Macro Cross-examination*: The opposing attorney will attack your entire field or total area of expertise. In doing so, he or she will attempt to discredit you, your testimony, and the field by relegating it to junk science status.
4. *Destructive Cross-examination*: The opposing attorney will attack your credentials. This can be the bloodiest battle of all, as it is fought inside the expert's territory. Your credentials are challenged as inadequate, and your weaknesses exposed. An academic expert is usually strong on theory and weak on experience. The practicing professional has the opposite problem — weak on theory while strong in experience.

> The examiner will attempt to differentiate your experience from the fact pattern in the case. Every case is different, so no one's experience exactly replicates the case. The attorney will try to overemphasize these small differences. The attorney may attempt to show that the other side's expert is better than you are. He or she may also try to portray you as a professional expert witness by demonstrating that you devote virtually all of your time to litigation. If the lawyer is successful, the perception that you are merely a professional witness may eradicate the jury's impressions of your fairness, objectivity, and impartiality. Further, if the opposing attorney can demonstrate that you have a consistent track record of testifying with the same opinion on a topic, he or she may be able to make the case that you are biased and therefore lack objectivity. Likewise, should you routinely testify in support of cases against large corporations, for example, the opposing attorney will try to convince the jury of your predisposition against all corporations in an effort to destroy your neutrality.

It can be hard not to take this personally. Keep in mind that the intent of the opposing attorney is to have you "blow your cool." Despite the natural psychological tendency to strike back or become defensive or argumentative, you must be dignified and controlled under these tough circumstances. The attorney's goal is to expose you as being sensitive to criticism and biased in your opinions. Once the examiner has pierced the veil of objectivity, he or she will exploit that opening you have allowed. Regardless of the technique used, the intent of the opposing attorney is to discredit or impeach you for bias, prejudice, lack of perception, or prior inconsistencies.

Unlike the rules governing direct examination, the cross-examining attorney is allowed to ask leading questions of the expert. By asking leading questions, the cross-examining attorney gains control of the examination. While the scope of cross-examination is generally limited to what was covered on direct examination, the trial judge has latitude in determining the scope of the questioning allowed.[33]

Lawyers like to pose hypothetical questions when cross-examining expert witnesses. A hypothetical question is one that assumes facts not in evidence, the answer to which requires a witness to guess or surmise the answer. The answer necessarily is an opinion. Hypothetical questions can help clarify your opinion, but they also can flush out inconsistencies or portray you as unreliable. The purpose for using hypothetical situations or questions is to set the stage to make a point sometime in the future, either with you or with an opposing expert. If the attorney can get you to agree with a line of facts or

[33] Sacks.

logic in a hypothetical situation and then apply the same line to the actual facts of the case, the attorney may be able to cast doubt on your testimony and/or credibility. Through your responses to the hypothetical question, you may have unwittingly reversed your opinion or agreed with an opposing expert. Simply put, hypothetical situations and/or questions signal danger — and opportunity.

When confronted with a hypothetical situation or question, you have several alternatives. You can answer directly and without qualification. This is the easiest and most expedient approach, but you risk losing the opportunity to explain how the hypothetical situation departs from the actual facts in evidence — which would make the hypothetical incredible, and not your opinion. You can decline to respond, but that will either make you look vulnerable, or cast doubt on the veracity of your opinion. The most successful approach will be to ask the cross-examining attorney to clarify the situation or question by providing the underlying assumptions to you, rather than you having to infer those assumptions. This approach has two purposes. First, by the time the opposing lawyer restates and explains the question, the jury may have lost interest in both the question and the point it was intended to make. Second and far more importantly, this tactic likely will crystallize the information the attorney is trying to elicit to cast doubt on your written opinion. You then have the opportunity to demonstrate the differences between the hypothetical and the facts in evidence and how they affect your opinion.

The opposing attorney may also waive the right to cross-examine a witness. This can be an effective tactic if the facts or opinions in the testimony are not in contention. Additionally, cross-examination may provide an opportunity for the expert to edify or reinforce his or her testimony. By waiving cross-examination, the attorney may send the message that the testimony of the witness is of little importance or impact. However, in the case of expert witness testimony, the right to cross-examine will rarely, if ever, be waived. By waiving cross-examination, the jury could conclude that the expert's direct testimony — and the expert — are beyond challenge. The jury expects cross-examination. "[The] decision must be based upon how damaging the direct testimony was and whether you have any ground to bring his opinion or the basis into question."[34]

Cross-examination need not be a purely defensive situation for the expert. When the examiner asks a question, you may have an opportunity to reinforce points made under direct examination. The jury has the opportunity to reinforce its understanding of your opinions. Do not let the examiner cut you off or limit your responses. You may have to answer a question

[34] Clifford, 432.

"yes" or "no," but you also have the right to explain your answer. You may not get the opportunity to explain during cross-examination, but if your attorney senses that clarification is necessary, he or she will probably conduct a re-direct examination. In any case, if the question posed to you on cross-examination cannot be answered with a simple "yes" or "no" then say so. The opposing lawyer may try to cut you off with "thank you, that's all," but you should persist in conveying your need to clarify, conveying to the jury that the attorney is not letting you be complete in your answer.

Jury Instructions and Closing Arguments

After all the witnesses have testified and the defense has rested its case, the jury must prepare for deliberating and arriving at the verdict. To assist the jury in this process, written instructions are provided to the jury by the judge, who explains the issues to be decided, the applicable laws to be considered, and what specifically must be proven. These instructions may be verbal or in writing. The underlying purpose of these instructions is to ensure that the jury decides the case pursuant to the applicable law, rather than according to any opinion of what the law should be. In addition to an explanation of the applicable law, the judge provides direction concerning the expert testimony. According to the Federal Jury Instruction Guide, jury instructions should include the following statement:

> If you should decide that the opinion of an expert witness is not based upon sufficient education and experience, or if you should conclude that the reasons given in support of the opinion are not sound, or that the opinion is outweighed by other evidence, you may disregard the opinion entirely.

"The effect of the expert's opinion is ordinarily as great or as small as the jury may wish it to be."[35]

Suggested jury instructions are prepared well in advance by the lawyers representing both sides and submitted to the judge. After reviewing the suggestions, the judge usually discusses the instructions with the attorneys in an attempt to resolve any differences. These discussions are conducted outside of the presence of the jurors, often in the judge's chambers. In order to maximize regular working hours for jury convenience, these discussions are often conducted after hours and sometimes very late at night.[36]

[35] Nunnally, 31.
[36] Rabinoff and Holmes.

After the judge has provided the jury instructions, the attorneys make their closing arguments. In direct contrast to opening statements, the defense provides the first closing argument, followed by that of the plaintiff, for civil cases, or prosecution, for criminal cases. Expert witnesses can give excellent feedback in preparation for the closing arguments. You can tell the lawyer what evidence appeared to be persuasive to the jury and what evidence was not. You can identify the weak points of the testimony or case and suggest statements that may address them. The key theories and expert opinions can be effectively summarized and tied together through the use of previously admitted trial exhibits during the closing argument.[37]

Like opening statements, closing arguments are not evidence, but unlike opening statements, closing arguments may draw conclusions and are designed to persuade the jury to accept the party's theory. Closing arguments are the lawyers' last messages to the jury — the final opportunity to provide the evidence and other supporting rationale for why the jury should find in their favor. During closing arguments, the attorneys will attempt to persuasively recap the salient points to reinforce their case positions and the themes they have presented. As with opening statements, the final summation and closing statement to the jury will influence the final verdict.[38]

Post-Trial Motions and Appeals

The case is not over until both sides agree it is over. Consequently, once the verdict is rendered, the attorneys may file various post-trial motions. For the most part, an expert will not be actively involved in this process. The most common post-trial motion is a request for a new trial because of some error of law or undue prejudice to which the lawyer objected at trial. Another common post-trial motion argues that the jury verdict is against the weight of the evidence, and therefore the judge should reverse the jury's decision. If these motions are not granted, the losing party usually has the right to appeal the decision to a higher court.

Usually, "no new evidence can be presented in the appeal process since the court will only consider evidence presented at the trial" and contained in the trial record. "However, there can be exceptions which could result in the appeals court ordering a new trial."[39] Be prepared. The appeals process can take years after the trial is over. Don't throw away any of the papers, references, or research used in the preparation of your opinions. Box and save them. You may be called on to evaluate the appellate briefs filed by both

[37] Rossi.
[38] Rabinoff and Holmes.
[39] Rabinoff and Holmes, 37.

sides for technical accuracy. Settlement negotiations may be recommended in which you may be asked to take part. During the post-trial period, both sides are weighing the costs of further litigation against the potential upside and downside risks. These talks quite often involve technical points that may rely upon your testimony or expertise.

In summary, the true effectiveness of an expert witness is tested in the trial setting. Any case can ultimately go to trial, and that is where all the preparation pays off and plays out in a real-life drama in real time.

Section III

The Art, Business, and Future of Expert Witnessing

If the world should blow itself up, the last audible voice would be that of an expert saying it can't be done.

—Peter Ustinov

7

The Art of Expert Witnessing

The meeting of two personalities is like the contact of two chemical substances: if there is any reaction, both are transformed.

—**Carl Jung**

Developing the Professional Relationship

To one degree or another, all experts rely on the attorney who hired them for the information necessary to do their work. Therefore, you should communicate frequently with the attorney to develop the necessary rapport. This may be a challenge. Generally, lawyers may not want to spend much time on a case at the beginning, as they have other cases in progress which may be closer to the trial phase. Many times you will have to do the pushing if you want to get an early start.

Your first duties are to explore the technical issues and to educate the lawyer. Recognize that the issues confronting you and the attorney with whom you are working are never black and white. Experts tend to gravitate to one point of view and negate dissenting opinions. Lawyers, on the other hand, live in a world of gray, where facts can be toned and shifted into various points of view. Be open to the lawyer's perceptions, and see how he or she construes the facts differently than you do.

Working on a case is usually an interactive process, with you and the lawyer exchanging questions and information. The lawyer has to instruct you on the precise legal standards that must be addressed and on any relevant tests followed in the specific jurisdiction in which the case is pending. You should work with the attorney in order to make sure your opinion will be admissible. Ultimately, you and the lawyer must work together in a professional relationship built on mutual trust and respect.

Maximizing Your Effectiveness

How can you maximize your effectiveness, whether in a consulting or a testifying role? This is the art of expert witnessing.

Practice

Nothing improves your ability to be an effective expert witness like practice. If you have never had to engage in public speaking or have only done so before a "friendly" audience, you must develop new skills to make you an effective witness. Find opportunities to participate in panel or roundtable discussions or other forums where you may be required to defend a particular position or which use a question-and-answer format.

Study

Study the legal system in more depth. Make some free time to go down to the local courthouse and sit in on a trial. Try to figure out what is going on. A trial involving a small automobile accident has many of the same characteristics as a large product liability suit. Watch the jury as the witnesses testify. Do your own critique. Make notes of the courtroom procedures you don't understand and strange words used, and then ask a lawyer friend to explain them.

Be Prepared

Being prepared is critically important in all phases of the litigation process. Poor preparation can not only jeopardize the case at hand and your chances of being retained for future engagements, but it can also result in personal and professional embarrassment and the loss of credibility. Your lack of preparation allows the opposing side to cast doubt — on the record — upon your opinions, methodologies, and conclusions. If you are fully prepared, you will be a better witness. You will also be able to better deal with the inevitable surprises that arise in a trial.

Understand the law that specifically applies to the case in which you are testifying. In every area of the law, there are cases with which the expert should be familiar. Ask your lawyer to identify and provide copies of the significant precedents that may apply to the aspects of the case which are relevant to your work. More knowledge makes a better expert. By understanding your strengths and weaknesses, as well as those of both sides of the case, you will be better prepared for testifying and cross-examination.

It is also critically important to know the composition of the jury. What are the education levels of the jury members? What do the jurors do for work? Ultimately, the jury is your audience. The more they relate to and like you, the more credible you will be and, as a result, the more impact your testimony will have. This phenomenon is known as "affinity bias."[1]

Be Professional

A good expert looks and acts dignified. He or she dresses in good taste, in similar fashion to the lawyers involved in the case. While you want to present yourself as a highly qualified expert, you should never succumb to the temptation to exaggerate your qualifications even to the slightest. You know what you know, and you also know what you don't know. Be truthful and forthright. If you try to be an expert in many areas, the odds are you will appear to the jury to be an expert in none. Remember, there is a fine line between impressing the jury and arrogance.

The first few minutes of direct examination are critical in establishing your relationship with the jurors. Make it a friendly time by establishing eye contact and by talking directly to them. Sit up and smile. Speak loudly and clearly and avoid jokes or anecdotes. If the judge interrupts the proceedings, listen to what he or she has to say and then proceed as instructed. It is never a good idea to speak when the judge is speaking.

On cross-examination, be polite to opposing counsel, but protect yourself and your reputation. You do have the right to answer fully any question that the opposing attorney asks. He may try to cut you off after your "yes" or "no" response. Break in and indicate you have more to say, and explain your answers. If necessary, with the permission of the court, step down from the witness box to point out an exhibit or chart that reinforces your point. Don't be afraid to answer "I don't know" or "I can't remember." Ask for clarification of questions you may not fully understand. Ask for definitions of terms you are unclear about to ensure that you and the examining attorney

[1] Steven Lubet, *Expert testimony: A guide for expert witnesses and the lawyers who examine them* (Boston: National Institute For Trial Advocacy, 1998), 26.

are talking about the same thing. Examine and re-read all documents before referring to or testifying about them. It is more impressive to be thorough than all-knowing.

Never argue with the opposing attorney. You only lose as your credibility suffers with the jury. Also, never let the attorney coax you into a personal attack on the opposing expert. If you do, the jurors will begin to think you are not the unbiased expert they were led to believe. Remember, you are there to win jurors, not to beat the opposing attorney.

Choose your words carefully. There is a tremendous difference in perception between the words "possible," "probable," and "plausible." Choose among these words carefully, and be sure that you express your meaning for each so that the jury understands exactly what you mean when you use them.

Be Organized

Well-organized answers are easier to follow and more likely to be understood and believed. Listen carefully to the question. When answering, speak in an organized fashion, using words and images to which the jury easily relates. In response to complex or probing questions, you should frame your answers in the following sequence: conclusion, explanation of the method you used to reach the conclusion, and examples or analogy to drive home the point.

Tell the Story

You need to leave the jurors with a logical story they will never forget. It needs to be a consistent picture that is intellectually and emotionally anchored. The jurors must feel and see, as well as understand, your contentions. Simplify your testimony to, at the most, two or three main points. You must decide on one overall story or picture, with several supporting snapshots — more than that and the jury will become confused as to what your main points were.

You must be able to tell the story in two ways at the same time. The technical story must hold up under attacks from the opposition and provide a record under appeal. You must also tell the story in terms the lay person can understand. It must be interesting and free of jargon. If you lose the jury's attention for any reason, it is difficult to revive it, and you will also lose big points for your side.

Show Emotion

To anchor your testimony in the emotions of the jurors, you must express some emotion in your testimony. You are not just a mechanical robot programmed to say what was noted in the prepared scripts. You feel more strongly about certain things than others. Those feelings need to surface and be shown. This does not mean emotional outburst, such as anger or tears. It does mean appropriate voice inflection, bearing, and facial expression. Make your main points with strength of conviction; use hand gestures to communicate sincerity and belief. There is nothing fake about showing emotion to buttress your main points. It alerts the jury that something important is being said and they had better pay attention.

Educate

Your role is to develop a common understanding of events. You interpret the complex and make it simple. Different jurors will interpret information differently. Repeat what you say in different ways. For example, you may describe a chemical reaction in terms of charged ions that are attracted to each other through electrical forces. Alternatively, you may create a metaphor of this phenomenon by describing the reaction as a marriage between a female who has a certain affinity for a male. You carry the metaphor through to arrive at the vision you are sponsoring.

You may also communicate with the jury nonverbally. The jury is as likely to judge you by the way you answer questions as through the content of your answers. Always maintain eye contact with the jurors. Listen to the questions that are posed to you, and think for a few moments before answering. When you answer, use a slow and measured tone that shows you are confident. Make your answers brief and to the point. If you maintain the jurors' attention and confidently answer the questions, the jurors will perceive you, and the opinions you give, as credible, and they will give great weight to what you say.

Create Vivid Visualizations

Visualization is your most difficult task. You must take technically complex issues and break them down into components easily understood by the jury. Consider bringing technology into the courtroom. If the case involves a piece of faulty equipment, use a computer-generated model, an illustration, or a videotape. Compare what you bring to some familiar, common object. An industrial boiler may become a teapot. A chemical reaction is like a pressure cooker. If you do a demonstration or simulation, make sure it works the way you planned. Nothing is worse than a bungled experiment on the witness stand.

Use words that bring vision to life in your oral testimony. Steel does not just lose strength though the erosive action of an abrasive substance, it *becomes weak* as the *sandpaper-like* material *eats away* at the metal. State the observations in technical terms, but then follow up with the visualization.

The Ethics of Expert Witnessing

Being an expert witness brings with it a great deal of responsibility. You must appreciate the pivotal role that you may play in a case. In a greater sense, you must also acknowledge that you represent your profession and associated professional organizations. It is imperative that you conduct yourself in a highly professional and ethical manner. The single most important piece of advice for expert witnesses is to tell the truth, simply and directly. This cannot be overemphasized.

But there is more to the ethics of expert witnessing than simply telling the truth. Too many experts agree to support a case without fully understanding how much of their time will really be necessary to do the job properly — ethically. If you are unwilling to work wholeheartedly on the case and to put in the time required to do the job correctly, don't accept the engagement. To accept under such circumstances is a clear breach of ethics in virtually any field or profession.[2]

You are ethically bound to be totally candid with your lawyer on the development of your opinions. Your attorney needs to develop strategies and tactics to deal with the weaknesses of the case that you identify. Of course, the lawyer is ultimately the spokesperson for his or her client and thus will want you to provide an opinion that most strongly supports winning the case. This is where the majority of ethical dilemmas arise.

Should you expose case weaknesses in the courtroom as a measure of your objectivity? To what degree should you be led by your attorney? Certainly, you should never cross the ethical boundary of stating opinions that are not yours or that you do not believe in, but should you withhold opinions or feelings that are detrimental to "your" side?

Usually, this dilemma can be resolved on direct examination. The attorney asks questions about the weaknesses so you have the opportunity, under a friendly situation, to explain how the weaknesses were dealt with in the opinion. The worst case is when the weaknesses are so great that they are potentially devastating to the client. In that instance, you and your attorney need to decide whether or not it is wise for you to testify at all. If the weaknesses are not brought out during direct examination, they most certainly will be under cross-examination. In that event, you lose a great deal of control. Watch how you frame your findings and explain your conclusions.

Finally, it is important to make clear that, as an expert, you are being "paid for the time to testify, not for the testimony."[3] If you are known for

[2] Eric Pierson, *1999 Wiley expert witness update: New developments in personal injury litigation* (Frederick, MD: Aspen Law and Business, 1999).

[3] John P. Coniglio, The expert witness: A primer on your activities, *Professional Safety*, (January 2002), 34–39.

your objectivity and honesty as an expert, you can be of great value in helping your lawyers successfully try and/or settle the case. "The single most important obligation of an expert witness is to approach every question with independence and objectivity."[4]

The Future of Expert Witnessing

In many ways, the future looks bright. Brilliant minds are graduating from law schools in increasing numbers, creating the potential for more litigation. The nature of litigation is more complex due to society's reliance on technology. Governmental regulations in the areas of health, safety, and environment are more voluminous. All these trends mean that experts will be relied on with greater frequency in coming years. Indeed, expert witnessing is a growth industry.

These trends, however, have also resulted in a clogged court system that is bogged down by too many cases and an all-too-often arduous trial process. For several years now, the idea of "tort reform" has been debated, and was, as of this writing, the subject of proposed Congressional legislation. The advent of no-fault insurance, which is essentially a soft form of tort reform enacted in some states to alleviate the legal harangue of accident-related suits and counter-suits, has resulted in a lowered number of personal injury lawsuits in those jurisdictions. Other ways of avoiding litigation, such as Alternative Dispute Resolution (ADR) are also being advocated. These moves away from the formal legal system will not only profoundly change the current system of tort litigation, but can also dramatically impact the need for, and alter the role of, experts.

Revisiting the Use of "Neutral" Experts

The American Bar Association (ABA) and the American Association for the Advancement of Science (AAAS) have initiated a "demonstrative project" aimed at testing and evaluating the use of neutral, court-appointed experts in federal cases. The primary emphasis of this project is to provide judges with an effective and expedient method for finding qualified scientists and engineers to hire as experts, rather than relying on word-of-mouth recommendations. According to Rule 706, especially in technical and complex litigation such as computer science, toxicology, and financial services, the

[4] Michael E. Sacks, *An overview of the law: A guide for testifying and consulting experts* (Horsham, PA: LRP Publications, 1995), 17.

court can appoint neutral experts, as opposed to those chosen by the parties, to effectively and impartially help assess and screen substantial amounts of often contradictory scientific data in order to prevent junk science from entering the courtroom. The specific role the neutral expert plays is determined on an individual, case-by-case basis.

While the notion of neutral experts has been around for more than a hundred years, few judges actually use this option. On the one hand, the premise of this project is that the use of neutral experts presents another option that could reduce costs and time spent on scientifically complex cases. Of course, the converse may also prove to be true. Each of the opposing sides may well rely even more substantially on experts in order to enhance the probability that the testimony proffered will support their side of the case.

Regardless of the ultimate effect, litigation is fast becoming more complex. Consequently, experts are increasingly the primary option for addressing today's technical and scientific complexity. Courts around the country are revisiting the role of court-appointed neutral experts.

The Impact of Technology

High technology continues to influence both the type of expert testimony introduced in court and the manner in which it is presented. The latest techniques in chemical analysis are carted into the courtroom even before standardization and total acceptance by the professional organizations. Genetic testing of humans through DNA analysis is one such method in widespread use in the legal system while still undergoing standardization in the profession. Novel theories of causation are flowing out of medical research. In toxic tort cases, the application of medical ecology theories based on damage to the human immune system by certain chemicals is controversial in the profession but has been accepted in several court jurisdictions. The application is based on the AIDS mode for immune system damage; instead of viruses attacking certain cells, chemicals do the damage. The field of forensic entomology used to date the deaths of humans based on the life cycles of maggots is quite different from its classical use to detect sources of insect infestation in civil cases. These and other revolutions in science will spin off directly to the experts who may be the ones fomenting change, or those who quickly recognize uses in forensics. Experts who do not keep up with the latest technological advances and theories in their fields may find themselves unused and unwanted.

The use of high technology in the courtroom as a means of communicating with the jury is also undergoing rapid change. The traditional blackboards, slides, posters, and scale models are being supplemented by videos and video animation. The incredible decrease in the cost of computer processing power and speed has directly translated into lowered costs of animation in the last few years. Animations formerly costing $1,000 per second now cost less than $100 per second. A riveting 2-minute video animation shown to a jury demonstrating exactly what happened and how your case is substantiated can cost less than $20,000 — a more-than-affordable price in cases where settlements or awards are in the million-dollar-plus range. "Modern jurors have grown up with television, and they believe and remember what they see. Advocates must realize digital imaging is the future, and the future is now. Today's jurors must be shown as well as told."[5]

Also, more courts are allowing video clips of alleged victims to be played to juries to show restrictions in their day-to-day activities as part of damages claims. Experts may become actors in small dramas played out in front of cameras, demonstrating various aspects of their cases. Today, in some cases, both parties agree to have their experts appear on tape and never show up in the courtroom. Experts who are comfortable operating in this highly technological environment will be in ever-increasing demand.

High-technology approaches, however, are not without pitfalls and limitations. In one case, the opposing expert and attorney put together an amazing display on direct examination. They had poster boards, slides, video, a scale model, a well-choreographed chalkboard discussion, and a beautifully rehearsed series of questions and answers, a very polished performance! When it was over, they even seemed to bow to the jury with wide smiles before they sat down. Then came cross-examination, and the demeanor of the expert changed. He stuttered and sputtered. He became angry and sarcastic. His earlier performance through all the slick high technology contrasted so dramatically with his cross-examination that his personal credibility — and, more importantly, the credibility of his testimony — suffered. As a postscript, the elegant scale model was not entirely wasted. The other side was able to use this model to refute the testimony of the opposing expert — yet another potential pitfall to be considered.

Alternative Dispute Resolution

The traditional litigation model is based on an adversarial system in which one party wins and the other loses. In the last decade, however, parties have

[5] Dean M. Harts, Reel to Real: Should you believe what you see?, *Defense Counsel Journal,* (October 1999), 514.

been turning to alternative forms of dispute resolution, usually by mutual agreement.

Arbitration and mediation are the primary forms of alternative dispute resolution (ADR). Arbitration typically involves a truncated presentation of facts and law before a panel of arbitrators chosen by the parties. The arbitrators may be attorneys specializing in the field of law implicated in the case, and in some cases are professionals in the relevant industry. Their decision is binding on the parties but usually takes into consideration that both sides have legitimate claims and explanations for how the dispute arose. Parties in arbitration are often more open to smaller damages awards in exchange for a less acrimonious and less costly process.

Mediation differs from arbitration in that the decision of a mediator is nonbinding. Often a mediator acts simply as a neutral party who engages in "shuttle diplomacy" to help the parties reach a settlement agreement. Some courts offer voluntary mediation programs in an effort to resolve cases before the parties become entrenched in litigation.

The increasing use of ADR is going to require the expert to develop broader skills. As parties look for common grounds and ways to work out differences, experts will not be scrutinized as closely as they are under *Daubert*. Experts for opposing sides may feel freer to acknowledge competing theories or methodologies.

Unlike trials, where judges and juries are not expected to know much about the subject matter of the cases they hear until the trial begins, arbitrators and mediators tend to be well-versed in the relevant field and so require less explanation of fundamental facts and circumstances. Therefore, experts play a different role in mediation and arbitration. Experts still have to read all documents, examine all evidence, and be ready for cross-examination. When acting as arbitrator or mediator, experts get different points of view (from witnesses). Experts serving as traditional witnesses have more flexibility within ADR. Rules in arbitration can be changed as long as the parties involved agree. Parties can agree to present testimony by document, affidavit, or deposition. Usually, experts do not have to testify in ADR proceedings, but they can be called for cross-examination. Arbitrators can ask questions and seek information from the other side which will not later haunt them in cross-examination. No juries are present in arbitration, so experts can be less formal, but they still have to study the facts of the case and give their opinion.

Tort Reform

Perhaps the area under current scrutiny that has the greatest potential impact upon expert witnessing is tort reform. Both sides of the argument present compelling rationale. The purpose of this section is not necessarily to add to the debate, but rather to describe the present and impending forces for change in tort law and to identify the potential implications for expert witnessing.

While the issue of tort reform is not new, the current debate is increasingly contentious and widespread. A recent editorial in *The Wall Street Journal* entitled "Damage Control" asserts that "America's tort system has become one of the most costly and inefficient methods of dispute resolution in the world, raising the costs of goods and services while reducing the availability of important products in the marketplace."[6]

Part of the call for tort reform is in response to the enforcement of seemingly antiquated, unbalanced and/or potentially obscure laws that tort reformers contend need to be reviewed, at the very least.

Proponents of tort reform also cite the increasing number of seemingly "frivolous" or even "nefarious" cases as a major contributor to the professed tort "crisis" in the United States.

Tort litigation has and continues to dramatically alter the range, availability, and cost of goods and services in industries ranging from health care and workplace safety to automobile leasing and fast food. As this trend continues, there will be increasing outcries of unfairness, capriciousness, and malfeasance. However, there are far too many examples and resultant cases where innocent people have greatly suffered for the neglect and/or intentional violation of the law regarding the discharge of toxic chemicals, exposure to unsafe working conditions and hazards, and inadequate product safety. The tort system was established to provide recourse for legitimate victims and to dissuade illegal injurious conduct. This is reason enough to for the proponents who staunchly support the system as it currently exists in the United States. Regardless of the outcome, it is clear that expert witnesses will have a significant role to play in the adjudication of tort cases.

Despite all the efforts to curtail tort litigation in all its mosaic form, these efforts can only decelerate the ever-growing needs of society to find redress in the court system. The technological complexities of our existence, coupled with the rapid pace of innovation, guarantee that experts will continue to be essential in resolving disputes. Those of you willing to pursue this novel use for your expertise will find, as I have, a love and respect for the legal system, despite its obvious shortcomings. As someone once stated about democracy: It isn't very efficient, but it beats all the other alternatives.

[6] C. Boyden Gray, "Damage control," *The Wall Street Journal*, December 11, 2002, A18.

8

The Business of Expert Witnessing

In this modern age, an expert is found in any field, no matter how esoteric.

The cost may be high to employ the expert, but it may well be higher not to employ one. Indeed, counsel who chooses to proceed without an expert may be flirting with malpractice.

—Melvin Belli

Perfecting the art of expert witnessing is essential if you are to successfully perform your part in litigating a case. Expert witnessing can be one of the most intellectually stimulating and fulfilling — or frustrating — activities in which you can participate. However, it is also extremely important to understand that an expert is an individual who renders services in exchange for compensation and, as such, needs to operate in a businesslike manner.

For some, expert witnessing provides full-time employment. For others, it provides supplemental income. In either case, an expert will need to consider a variety of issues associated with the business of expert witnessing.

Expert Witness Liability

The concept of witness immunity originated in English common law to encourage open and honest testimony without fear of reprisals or subsequent lawsuit based on the testimony provided. This principle was subsequently adopted by the American judicial system. Preservation of witness immunity has been so important that it has been maintained even where a witness was potentially negligent, as evidenced in the Texas Appeals Court opinion in the case of *Clark v. Grigson*. The Court stated "that no civil liability exists on the part of an expert witness who forms an opinion and states that opinion in the course of his testimony in a judicial proceeding, even though he may have been negligent in the process."[1]

The United States Supreme Court confirmed the importance of witness immunity through opinions rendered in two cases in the 1980s. The opinion in the 1983 case of *Briscoe v. LaHue* stated that "a witness who knows that he might be forced to defend a subsequent lawsuit, and perhaps to pay damages, might be inclined to shade his testimony in favor of the potential plaintiff, to magnify uncertainties, and thus to deprive the finder of fact of candid, objective and undistorted evidence."[2] Subsequently, in the 1985 case of *Mitchell v. Forsyth*, the Supreme Court stated that "the judicial process is an arena of open conflict, and in virtually every case, there is, if not always a winner, at least one loser. It is inevitable that many of those who lose will pin the blame on…witnesses and will bring suit against them in an effort to relitigate the underlying conflict."[3]

While there is support and precedent for witness immunity, there is also a growing desire for increased accountability of experts, in large part as a result of the tremendous proliferation of expert testimony in tort litigation over the past 30 years.[4] Expert accountability is important because paid experts influence juries. This contention was substantiated in a poll conducted in the early 1990s by the *National Law Journal* and LexisNexis. The results showed that 89% of the criminal and civil jurors sampled found paid experts believable.[5] As the use and influence of expert witnesses increases, and as the financial stakes of litigation grow significantly, pressure will increasingly mount for holding experts accountable for the accuracy and validity of their testimony.

[1] *Clark v. Grigson*, 579 S.W.2d 263 (Tx. 1978).
[2] *Briscoe v. LaHue*, 460 U.S. 325 (1983).
[3] *Mitchell v. Forsyth*, 472 U.S. 511 (1985).
[4] E.G. Jensen, When "hired guns" backfire: the witness immunity doctrine and the negligent expert witness, *University of Missouri at Kansas City Law Review* (1993), 62, 185–210.
[5] Joan M. Cheever and Joanne Naiman, The view from the jury box, *National Law Journal*, (February 22, 1993).

Certain mechanisms built into the legal system ensure honest and accurate expert testimony; however, the effectiveness of these mechanisms is suspect in light of the nature of expert testimony in current tort litigation. The first and most obvious of the systemic mechanisms is cross-examination. Theoretically, the cross-examining attorney has two opportunities to challenge an expert's testimony. The first of these opportunities presents itself in the *Daubert* hearing, where the purpose is to challenge the methodology employed by the expert. The second opportunity is, of course, during cross-examination at the trial. Unlike the *Daubert* hearing, where the expert's methodology is in question, cross-examination during trial is primarily aimed at either impeaching the witness's credibility or discrediting the facts and conclusions presented by the expert.

However, most cross-examining attorneys are ill-prepared to adequately undermine a credible and well-prepared expert witness, not through lack of intellect but rather due to the lack of scientific, medical, or technical education and background. Experienced experts understand the legal system, the intent of cross-examination, and most importantly, the nuances and significance of the facts and their findings in a case. Based on this depth of understanding, an experienced expert usually remains calm, focused, and consistent under cross-examination. "Searching cross-examination may not yield any other result than to provide an opportunity for the expert witness to repeat his already damaging testimony."

The second primary systemic mechanism for ensuring reliable and accurate testimony is the potential prosecution for perjury. As in the case of cross-examination, however, this mechanism is also suspect. In the 1984 case *Sears v. Rutishauser,* the Illinois Supreme Court recognized that "it is virtually impossible to prosecute an expert witness for perjury...[T]he opinion is the result of reasoning, and no one can be prosecuted for defective mental processes."[6] In a similar opinion, the Wyoming Supreme Court found in *Little v. Kobos* that,"a witness is not guilty of perjury simply because his testimony is inconsistent...[I]nternal inconsistencies in testimony or an insufficient foundation for the basis of an expert's opinion...may provide sufficient contradiction to allow the jury to disregard the opinion rendered...."[7] Based on these opinions, faulty reasoning, inconsistent testimony or a lack of foundation for an expert's testimony may render an expert ineffective — and therefore not appealing to potential clients — but these are not sufficient basis for perjury.

While prosecution for perjury may be difficult, that does not mean there are no other punitive actions to which an expert may be subjected. In a June 2001 ruling, the U.S. Circuit Court of Appeals for the Seventh Circuit held

[6] *Sears v. Rutishauser* 466 N.E. 2d 210, 212 (Ill. Sup. Ct. 1984).
[7] *Little v. Kobos* 877 P.2d 752 (Wy. Sup. Ct. 1994).

that a member of a professional society could be disciplined by that society for improper testimony. In that case, a neurosurgeon sued the American Association of Neurological Surgeons for suspending him as a result of his expert testimony on behalf of the plaintiff in a medical malpractice suit. The doctor's suspension was upheld by both the district court and the appellate court on the basis that the testimony provided was irresponsible and that it violated the society's code of ethics.[8]

In addition to experts being at risk for discipline by professional societies, some courts have allowed lawsuits to be brought against expert witnesses.[9] One such example is the 1992 case *Murphy v. A.A. Matthews*, in which the Missouri Supreme Court found that professional experts were not protected from negligence lawsuits on the basis of witness immunity. In this case, the plaintiff alleged that incompetence and carelessness on the part of experts retained in support of its original case directly led to the inability to obtain appropriate compensation through that litigation. The defense cited witness immunity as protection from liability for the experts; based upon this contention, the trial court dismissed the case. Upon review, however, the Missouri Supreme Court reversed the dismissal on a basis similar to the standard-of-care doctrine applicable in legal malpractice, indicating that experts should receive consistent treatment, and that experts should be subject to the same level of negligence liability when providing expert testimony to the court as they would be in the normal conduct of their other professional work. The Court viewed experts as advisors and advocates rather than as objective and independent witnesses. Because the engineering firm charged a fee and voluntarily agreed to provide expert services to assist the claim of the plaintiff, professional standard of care was assumed, and witness immunity did not apply.[10]

The implications are clear. An individual who undertakes expert witness work without receiving adequate training and who does not understand the standards of practice for forensic evaluations, report writing, and testimony might be subject to a claim that he or she performed the work negligently and was responsible for any unfavorable judgment.[11]

[8] Renee L. Binder, Liability for the psychiatrist expert witness, *The American Journal of Psychiatry*, (November 2002), 1819–1825.
[9] Mary V. Moore, Gary G. Johnson and Deborah F. Beard, Liability in litigation support and court testimony: Is it time to rethink the risks? *Journal of Legal Economics* (1999), 53–63.
[10] *Murphy v. A.A. Mathews* 841 S.W. 2d 671 (Missouri, 1992).
[11] Binder, 1819–1825.

Forming an Expert Witnessing Business

The potential liability for negligent expert testimony raises the fundamental question of the best way to conduct business as an expert witness. Generally speaking, the risk of potential liability leads most businesses to operate as a separate entity from the principals involved. The most common such entity is the corporation. A corporation is a separate and distinct legal entity. It can open a bank account, pay taxes, and own property. The primary advantage of a corporation is that the owners or stockholders of the corporation are not personally liable for the debts and liabilities of the corporation. For example, if a corporation gets sued and is forced into bankruptcy, the owners will not be required to pay the debt with their own money, unless the owners have personally guaranteed the debt. If the assets of the corporation are not enough to cover the debts, the creditors cannot go after the stockholders, directors, or officers of the corporation to recover any shortfall.

The decision as to the best type of corporation is significant and has potentially far-reaching legal, reporting, and tax implications. The advice of a business and/or tax attorney, as well as that of an accountant, is imperative in deciding which type of business organization to adopt. Following are the four primary types of corporate or corporate-like entities available to the expert:

General Corporation

A general corporation, also known as a "C" corporation, is one of the most common corporate structures. A general corporation may have an unlimited number of stockholders. Because a general corporation is a separate legal entity, a stockholder's personal liability is usually limited to the amount of investment in the corporation and no more, except in the case of fraud or negligence.

Close Corporation

A close corporation may be most appropriate for an individual starting a company alone or with a small number of people. While similar to a general corporation, a close corporation is limited to only thirty stockholders. In addition, many close corporation statutes provide existing stockholders the right of first refusal to purchase shares of the corporation before selling to new stockholders. The close corporation is not recognized in all states.

Subchapter S Corporation

A Subchapter S corporation is a general corporation that has elected a special tax status with the Internal Revenue Service. Subchapter S corporations are most appropriate for small-business owners and entrepreneurs who prefer to be taxed as if they were still sole proprietors or partners. When a general corporation makes a profit, it pays a federal corporate income tax on that profit. If the corporation also declares a dividend, the stockholders must report the dividend as personal income and pay additional personal income and/or dividend taxes. S Corporations avoid this "double taxation" (once at the corporate level and again at the personal level) because all income or loss is reported only once on the personal tax returns of the stockholders. For many small businesses, the S Corporation offers the best of both worlds, combining the tax advantages of a sole proprietorship or partnership with the limited liability and enduring life of a corporate structure. The S Corporation does have certain restrictions, however. These restrictions and/or requirements include the following:

1. All stockholders must be citizens or permanent residents of the United States.
2. The maximum number of stockholders for an S Corporation is 75.
3. If an S Corporation is held by an "electing small business trust," then all beneficiaries of the trust must be individuals, estates, or charitable organizations. Interests in the trust cannot be purchased.
4. S Corporations may only issue one class of stock.
5. No more than 25% of the gross corporate income may be derived from passive income.

Limited Liability Company (LLC)

An LLC is not actually a corporation, but it offers many of the same advantages. Limited liability companies are a relatively new type of business entity that combines the limited liability protection of a corporation with the "pass through" taxation of a sole proprietorship or partnership. The LLC form is available in all 50 states and Washington, D.C., and has the following additional advantages over "C" or "S" corporations:

- allows greater flexibility in management and business organization, and
- does not have the ownership restrictions of S Corporations, making an LLC an ideal business structure for foreign investors.

Contractual Considerations for Expert Witnesses

Consider using a formal contract, drafted either by you or by the attorney hiring you, to memorialize the scope of your engagement. If there is some reluctance on the part of the lawyer to enter into a formal contractual relationship, send a memorandum of understanding with the terms spelled out so that you each have a record. A contract is not essential if the client is already paying the bills, the relationship is a happy one, or both parties agree that a contract is not necessary; however, a contract can be key if things go sour.

On the other hand, some attorneys prefer not to have an actual contractual agreement in place because such agreements are discoverable under Rule 26 (b) (1). "Contractual documents recording the hiring of an expert's services by counsel are discoverable if found relevant to the claim's subject matter. Relevancy is more liberally interpreted in the discovery phase and is not restricted to merely admissible evidence."[12] The decision to have a written contract must be made on a case-by-case basis, depending on the length of time and the closeness of the professional relationship between the expert and the attorney.

Basic Types of Contractual Arrangements

You can use several basic types of contractual agreements in the conduct of business as an expert witness. It is important to note that contingency contracts — contracts where the compensation of the expert relies on success in the litigation or settlement and the size of the award — are not recommended in any circumstance. Most jurisdictions prohibit expert compensation from being dependent on either the content of the testimony or the outcome of the case. Even in the jurisdictions that allow contingency compensation, the credibility of the expert and his or her testimony is highly vulnerable when — not if — the terms of the expert's compensation are disclosed to the jury. It is difficult to convince a jury that you are objective when you have a stake in the outcome.

Retainer Contracts

This type of contract provides for an advance payment — retainer — that gives you partial payment at the outset of the engagement, rather than billing as or after work is performed. A retainer typically ranges from 10 to 33% of the total estimated fee of the entire engagement. For clarity, a post-retainer fee basis and payment schedule should be provided.

In certain circumstances, an expert may require the entire fee in advance. This type of relationship is rare and relies on a variety of factors, such as the

[12] Robert. D. Fleming, Hazards of expert witnesses: Disclosing work product and limiting testimony, *Defense Counsel Journal*, (October, 1999), 538–554.

demand for and capabilities of the expert involved, the magnitude of the case, and the importance of the expert to the success of the litigation, to name a few.

If, for any reason, you have doubt as to whether or not you will get paid or you need an advance to get started, require a retainer. For example, an out-of-state lawyer inquires about using you in a case. You are not familiar with the law firm or the client. You might ask for a retainer as a matter of course. You will find out quickly how seriously interested they are in having you participate in their case. If they send you an advance and never use you, then you have the right to keep it, as long as your contract with them does not specify otherwise.

Retainers are also used as a means of securing an expert so he or she is unavailable to support other parties in the litigation. In this case, retainers are normally non-refundable. Do not feel guilty about keeping all or part of the retainer. The parties may have settled the case partially by using your name as leverage during the negotiation. "The fee also serves as payment to the forensic expert for use of his name in the disclosure document that will be given to the opposing counsel."[13]

Time and Materials Contracts

In this type of contract, the fees are calculated on the basis of how much time was committed to the case and what materials, services, and other costs were actually incurred. Some experts charge differential fees based on the nature of the work performed. Testifying and depositions are far more demanding and therefore usually command a higher price than preparation and research. Reimbursable expenses — such as out-of-pocket costs, including copying costs, expenses associated with building models or conducting experiments, and travel expenses — can be substantial, and the responsibility for payment should be clearly defined. A time and materials contract with an initial retainer is widely considered the most appropriate type of contract for expert witnessing.

Flat Fee Contracts

In this type of contract, you are compensated a negotiated, pre-determined fee that is all-inclusive for either the entire engagement or for specifically defined portions thereof. As a result, this type of contract has a great deal of inherent risk for both parties, but especially for you, the expert. This type of contract is unacceptable unless your work product and delivery schedule are extremely well-defined. For example, the discovery process is virtually always

[13] Marc A. Rabinoff and Stephen P. Holmes, *The forensic expert's guide to litigation: The anatomy of a lawsuit* (Horsham, PA: LRP Publications, 1996).

full of surprises that make accurate cost estimation difficult. Trials get rescheduled, and venues for discovery and deposition change. If you elect to use a flat fee contract, it should clearly spell out all of the terms of the agreement.

Usually, law firms have form consulting contracts; however, if they do not, you can construct one yourself. It can be relatively simple, but it is beneficial to run the proposed contract past an attorney representing your business to make sure it meets legal requirements. The agreement or contract should address and include seven main elements: term, fees and expenses, billing and payment terms, confidentiality, conflict of interest, statement of work, and termination. Regardless of who drafts it, make sure you fully understand all the terms and conditions of the contract.

Term of the Agreement

This is the period of time for which the contract is in effect. The agreement usually starts on the date the contract is executed — signed by representatives of the parties involved — and ends when the case is over, whether by settlement or exhaustion of legal remedies. Alternately, the parties may include specific start and end dates.

Fees and Expenses

Fees should be set at levels that meet your financial needs and are reasonable for your field and level of expertise. Fees can be based on a variety of criteria, including the following:

- Formal education
- Professional positions held
- Practical experience directly in the field of study or discipline
- Practical experience as an expert witness
- Publications, including books, articles, texts, and interviews
- Name recognition and reputation as an expert

Fees for science, engineering, and technical experts commonly range from $100 to $300 per hour. Medical and psychological experts can command up to $500 per hour, or more. Experts are differentiated by their abilities and track records, not by the fees charged, unless those fees are extremely high or low. Extremely low fee levels can give the impression that the expert does not feel very qualified or lacks confidence. Extraordinarily high fee levels can indicate arrogance or an unwillingness to provide expert testimony unless extremely well compensated.

Regardless of the level, fees should be consistent for all your clients. However, you can establish a range of fees that depends on the nature of the effort to be expended. Some experts add a service charge to cover administrative expenses. Others charge the same hourly or daily fee, regardless of the type of service and without any service charges. Some experts charge a premium of 100 to 200% of their basic rate for testifying, on the basis of the heightened stress and time-consuming nature of trial and deposition appearances. Others consider the actual time spent testifying is but a fraction of the total effort, and therefore no premium is charged. Some experts require the payment of a non-refundable fee at the outset of every engagement as compensation for agreeing to forego retention by other parties in the litigation. Regardless of the basis, consistent and fair prices that position you to attract the desired level of work are best in the long run.

It is common practice for lawyers to request a rough estimate for the projected level of effort that you would have to spend on a particular case. The general rule of thumb is to estimate the number of hours and the amount of travel, support, and other miscellaneous charges and multiply it by a factor of two or three in an attempt to cover the many unforeseen contingencies. A schedule of standard fees that forms the basis for estimating the total cost of an engagement should include the following:

1. Direct Labor (rate per hour)
   - Testifying witnesses
     - Report preparation
     - Research
     - Deposition
     - Testifying
   - Nontestifying witnesses
   - Other experts
   - Graphics and visual aid developers
   - Research support
2. Miscellaneous Services
   - Outside services (other consultants or subcontractors)
   - Rental or construction of special equipment
   - Construction of models or exhibits
   - Storage of evidence
3. Travel and Miscellaneous Charges
   - Transportation (airfare, mileage, parking, taxis, etc.)

Lodging and meals
Telephone charges
Mail, overnight delivery service, fax, and/or courier services

All estimates should include the appropriate hourly rates, the rates of assistants, and the number of billable hours for travel time. A reasonable way to bill travel time is to charge the client half the normal hourly rate (or for up to 4 hours). Additionally, you should identify the cost of travel or a provision that ensures reimbursement of "fair and actual" travel expenses. Charge for personal car use can be included, if appropriate; you can use the reimbursement rate stipulated by the Internal Revenue Service for the cost of operating and maintaining an automobile for tax purposes. Specify whether the client will pay for business- or first-class air travel expenses. Specify processing or administrative fees if such fees are applicable and incurred. For lengthy cases — those that have a high probability of lasting for more than a year — include a clause that allows you to change the rates with, say, 30 days' notice.

It is also important to be prepared to explain that you are being paid, and what you are being paid, for your efforts and for rendering an opinion. In the last decade, expert fees have risen dramatically as lawyers have depended more heavily on experts. However, you may be accountable to the court for the reasonableness of the fees you are paid. For example, under the California Code of Civil Procedure section 2034(i)(4), an expert must provide: (1) proof that the expert has charged and been paid similar fees for providing similar services before, (2) the total number of times the fee has been charged and received, and (3) the regularity with which the expert has received the desired fee over the two years preceding any hearing on the motion. Reasonableness is not meant to be synonymous with what an expert has "customarily" charged. Some jurisdictions have specific local rules regarding the fees an expert can charge the opposing side, such as in the case of deposition.[14]

Billing and Payment Terms

"According to experts from a variety of fields, bills for experts' services often end up at the bottom of attorneys' priority lists. The best way to ensure payment is to require a retainer up front."[15]

It is important to have a schedule that spells out your billing practices and delineates the billing frequency. Normally, the bill should contain time

[14] Elizabeth J. Cohen, Don't take experts from strangers, *ABA Journal* (April 2002).
[15] Experts get strict on billing procedures, *The Testifying Expert* (September 1994), 6.

sheets for you and your assistants, showing the date, hours spent, and a brief description of the work performed. The invoice should also provide a detailed list of all expenses other than labor which are being submitted for reimbursement. Expenses can be billed at cost or with a small service fee, usually ten percent. When a retainer is involved, you bill against the retainer amount; after it is exhausted, either ask for another retainer or keep billing. For flat-fee contracts, a payment schedule should also be provided. It is a good idea to receive all payments in full for activities prior to testimony in depositions and trial.

You may set your own schedule for billing. Billing on a monthly basis is standard. Getting paid should also be regular; however, the rate is generally slower for any or all of the following reasons. First, lawyers understand the time value of money and like to hold on to it. Second, they often have to send the bill to the client or insurance company, which takes time. Third, they want to have the case settled and pay you out of the "pot." However, a good reason for lawyers to pay you promptly is to keep you motivated to give their case a high priority. All of us enjoy working more for lawyers who fully appreciate our work and show it with a quick response to the bill.

An important side note: Many jurisdictions have statutes stipulating that, if a written offer to settle an action is not accepted and the opposing side fails to obtain a more favorable judgment through litigation, the costs of the litigation may not be recovered. In some circumstances, the court may even require the unsuccessful party to pay the costs incurred by the opposing side. This includes actual and reasonable expenses associated with an expert witness in either trial preparation, or the trial itself.[16]

"Most experts get shortchanged for three reasons: They don't get an adequate retainer, they don't bill often, or the case settles while the expert is still working on it."[17] According to Dennis A. Toaspern, "All experts can possibly be contacted by both sides. Any of my conversations with attorneys are stopped as far as technical matters go until I've got a retainer and am actually working on the case."[18]

Confidentiality

Law firms will require that you agree not to discuss the case with anyone not specified by them. You can, however, get written permission if there is a

[16] Robert C. Clifford, *Qualifying and attacking expert witnesses*, (Santa Ana: James Publishing Group, 1990).
[17] Attorney's comment about fees spurs experts' reaction, advice, *The Testifying Expert*, (June 1996), 3.
[18] Watch out for conflict-of-interest traps set by some lawyers, *The Testifying Expert*, (March 1997), 4.

compelling reason to discuss the case with others. It is safest to assume that communications with either the client or retaining counsel may be subject to discovery. According to the American Bar Association Standing Committee on Professional Conduct, retention agreements "should define the relationship, including its scope and limitations, and should outline the responsibilities of the testifying expert, especially regarding the disclosure of client confidences."[19]

Your work product may be the property of the law firm, in which case it cannot be copied, sold, or published if so specified in the contract. Generally speaking, work leading to and including expert testimony does not fall within the ordinary practice of a profession.

Conflict of Interest

You have a conflict of interest as an expert when you are unable to provide impartial and objective focus and support to one client or issue as the result of previous or current involvement or connection with one or more other clients or issues. Operating in a conflict-of-interest situation will most often damage your credibility and weaken, if not destroy, the case of the side you are supporting. Even if there is only the appearance of a conflict, it is prudent to refrain from taking on the new engagement.

For expert witnesses, conflicts of interest primarily arise in three different situations. The first concerns the potential of an expert to be concurrently engaged for a party in one case and opposed to that same party in another. The second situation concerns the ability of an expert to switch sides at some point during litigation. The third situation, and perhaps the most common, is the use of client confidential or "inside" information gleaned from one case in a different one.

Unfortunately, there is no single sanctioning body or professional association for expert witnesses. As a result, there is no widely accepted code of ethics for expert witnesses. Most professional associations and/or professional societies, however, do have codes of ethics that can be applied to members' actions when performing as an expert in litigation, and these codes are being applied as a basis for standard-of-care consideration in the courts. Between 1980 and 1999, there was "a dramatic increase in the use of the American Medical Association's Code of Medical Ethics in judicial rulings concerning the medical profession. Of the 225 legal citations of the Code since 1943, 181 occurred between the years 1980 and 1999. These statistics underscore trends of significance for the medical profession — the societal

[19] Steven Lubet, *Expert testimony: A guide for expert witnesses and the lawyers who examine them* (Boston: National Institute For Trial Advocacy, 1998), 176.

trend of increased medical litigation and the judicial trend of relying on professional statements of conduct as standards of legal evaluation and judgment. In effect, the Code is evolving into an expert witness for professional conduct and as such is essential knowledge for practicing physicians."[20]

Beyond the various codes of ethics that may apply, the law of agency requires that you refrain from exploiting one client's confidences for the benefit of another. The absence of a code of ethics for expert witnesses reinforces the need for negotiating a mutually agreeable conflict-of-interest agreement and/or resolution between you and the attorney.[21]

It is best to resolve conflict-of-interest issues at the beginning of your involvement in any case. Set down ground rules to ensure that the conversation you have now with the attorney won't cost you a chance to do other work. Some attorneys will want to divulge confidential information about a case that would disqualify you from working for the opposition. You may want to halt the discussion by telling the attorney that — as much you'd like to help — you do not want to hear any confidential information.

Setting up the ground rules before the conversation gets too specific does carry an element of risk. You may alienate attorneys who are simply going about the business of trying to find the best experts for their cases.

Statement of Work

This part of the contract details what efforts you are being retained to perform and, most often, a tentative schedule for the delivery of those efforts. The statement of work may specify that you will make a written report, testify at deposition and trial, and generally be available for consultation. At the beginning of your work, you may be strictly a consultant. You will remain one until you are formally divulged to the opposing side, at which time you become a testifying expert. In some situations, you may remain a consulting expert and work strictly inside the case, never appearing in court (e.g., you have a potential conflict of interest with being a testifying expert but the firm wants the benefit of your expertise).

Termination

Language should be added to allow you or the law firm to terminate the agreement with thirty days' written notice while you are a consulting expert. Once you are designated a testifying expert, you will have great difficulty

[20] Karen Geraghty,. The code as expert witness, (October 2001), www.ama-assn.org.
[21] Lubet.

terminating your contract due to the prejudice that could result. You can put in a provision for arbitration arising from any disputes about the contract, such as work-related issues or timely payments of bills.

Marketing

As an expert, you will market your skills and expertise to lawyers who try cases in your area of expertise. Most experts are retained through the joint effort of the lawyer and the client.

Generally, the attorney and client will develop a list of experts. The attorney will make the final decision, with the consent of the client. As a result, your marketing strategy must be two-pronged, aimed both at attorneys and at your own profession. You need to have a marketing strategy that represents your expertise in the highest professional way. Lawyers want the best experts they can afford, and "best" includes your professionalism. The way you market yourself will form the initial impression potential clients will have of you.

Most likely, you have established a reputation as an expert in your profession. But is it known that you want to be an expert witness? In your normal dealings with colleagues, you can indicate your availability if the opportunity arises. Ask your current clients if they have pending or ongoing litigation, what attorneys they use, and if they know of lawsuits in your area of expertise. Let the word out and reinforce your interest without being obnoxious. Note, however, that your recommendation by the attorney's client must be above reproach. "An excellent approach, but the attorney must make sure that such recommendation will not become troublesome later on since the relationship between the client and expert must be purely professional to avoid any conflicts of interest."[22]

Consider the following methods of connecting with potential clients:

Organizational Directories

Investigate the criteria for listing yourself in various local and national organizational directories, both general and specific to your area of expertise. Among these are the American Bar Association's register of expert witnesses. The Defense Research Institute, a Chicago-based organization of attorneys, has established an expert witness index. A forensic services directory is maintained by the National Forensic Center, which also supplies lists of experts to Westlaw's computer-based forensic services directory.

[22] Rabinoff and Holmes, 3.

Professional Societies

Some professional organizations maintain lists of members available and specially qualified to serve as experts. For example, a listing in *Engineers of Distinction: A Who's Who in Engineering* may prove helpful for engineers. Seek and maintain membership in professional societies. Investigate the methods they use to handle inquiries from the general public regarding availability of qualified experts. Make sure those who respond to such inquiries have your up-to-date *curriculum vitae*. The key consideration is your active membership and participation within the organization.

Expert Witness Service Companies

Some firms match attorneys and other prospective clients with appropriate consultants. These firms will usually be listed in the Yellow Pages under the category "Attorney Service Bureau," or something similar. While use of these agencies represents an increased cost to the attorney and client, the expense may be justified by the efficiency of the search. The expert benefits from such a service in that the broker finds the referral and manages the administrative details. The services will add a 10 to 20% fee on top of your rate; this fee is paid by the attorney. When working with these firms, however, you should evaluate each case independently, declining those that are inappropriate to your expertise. Be wary of firms that charge you a fee to register or a finder's fee. Those fees should be collected from the client.

Networking

Get involved. Become politically active. Attend city council meeting concerning matters of interest to you or which involve some aspect of your specialty. Be prepared to interject your point of view. Become a familiar face in the political arena — where there's politics, you'll find attorneys. Such participation can provide exposure to potential consumers of your services while you shape your own environment through politics. Utilize your current networking techniques to spread the word that you are interested in providing expert testimony. Word-of-mouth advertising is a very effective marketing tool. "Most forensic experts who are well-known in the field became well-known first by personal referral."[23]

Letters to Attorneys

An important target of your efforts must be the attorneys themselves. If you do not have any direct contacts, consider asking friends and associates who

[23] Harold A. Feder, *Succeeding as an expert witness: Increasing your impact and income* (New York: Van Nostrand Reinhold, 2000), 39.

do to make an introduction. Once you have served as an expert witness, your client attorney can be a source of referrals to others. Attorneys know that the most effective method of finding the best forensic expert is to tap into other attorneys' personal experience in seeing the expert perform. Knowing the expert's integrity, ability to teach, and present opinions to the court, as well as personality and attitude are critical. A referring attorney can best judge these traits. "Most experienced trial lawyers resort to expert witnesses with whom they have worked in the past or about whom they learn though word of mouth from colleagues."[24]

Advertising

"The availability of expert witnesses can be seen in the pages of classified ads in every law journal."[25] Advertising in such journals is expensive, but the results can make it worthwhile. In preparing an advertisement, review the content and appearance of ads in the current issues of journals that target the specific audience you are trying to reach. Placement, wording, and overall appearance of any advertisement are all extremely important if your ad is to be effective. If your budget, level of training, and expertise justify the expense, consultation with an advertising firm that specializes in the legal area is advisable. The Internet is another possibility. Establish your own web site, and use the web address on your stationery, business card, and advertising.

While the potential benefits of advertising are fairly obvious, there is a downside to be considered. Advertising allows opposing attorneys the opportunity to claim that, by soliciting work rather than being sought out, you may be a "hired gun" who is biased and motivated to advocacy by money. Such contentions, whether valid or not, can diminish your credibility and potentially reduce the number of engagements you attract.

Direct Mail

Also direct, but less expensive, is a mail campaign aimed at the larger firms, which commonly maintain a catalog of known expert witnesses. One way to begin is to send out a brief letter (snappy but informative) with a current resumé or *vita* and perhaps a few business cards. Although you may receive only three or four inquiries from a mailing of 500, that response may be enough to justify your investment.

For a mailing, names and addresses can be collected from a variety of sources. The Yellow Pages telephone book in larger metropolitan areas will

[24] Knox D. Nunnally, Use of experts, (A State Bar of Texas seminar paper appearing in The Professional Development Program book *Advanced Personal Injury Law Course*, 1987), 32.
[25] Mark Crane, How do expert witnesses get away with lying?, *Medical Economics*, (January 11, 1999), 152–164.

categorize law firms by the type of law practiced. State and local bar associations print directories and yearbooks that are useful resources. For example, the state bar association publishes a legal directory that is on file even in small firms and may be found in the local law library. Most state and local associations print a yearbook. Some state associations sell lists of licensed attorneys organized by categories.

If you wish to solicit business in another state, contact that state's bar association regarding availability of address lists. Another good source is the *Martindale-Hubbell Law Dictionary.* Medium-sized and larger firms are usually subscribers to this yearly publication; you might obtain a copy through an attorney friend or the local public library.

Expert Referral Agencies

These agencies usually require experts to work exclusively through their agency for billing, retainers, and other financial agreements regarding any one case. Additionally, there is usually a fee associated with the use of referral agencies. Sometimes the retaining party pays this fee; other times the expert is responsible. This may be an effective marketing method for an expert who is just starting to practice as an expert witness, so long as the agreement with the agency is not overly restrictive and it is not for too long a period of time.

Marketing yourself in the highest professional manner is essential. The marketing effort must be systematic and regular. Lawyers hire experts when the need arises. Every three to six months, the legal community needs to know about your services. Make sure they know who you are and what you can do. Persistence, one of the attributes that made you an expert, will make you a sought-after expert witness.

Education-Based Marketing Strategies

As the number of experts proliferates and as attorneys become inundated with promotional materials from experts, the traditional methods of marketing are becoming less effective. An effective complement or alternative to traditional marketing is the use of education-based marketing strategies. Education-based marketing positions you as an authority by promoting your knowledge, rather than your services. An additional benefit to this approach is that it reinforces the expert's ability to effectively educate the jury and court — a fundamentally important skill requisite to successful litigation.[26] "Education-based marketing steers clear of hard-sell tactics.

[26] Market your expertise, not your products, *The Testifying Expert,* (February 1996), 1, 4.

Because of this fact, education-based marketing is the fastest growing and purest form of marketing."[27]

Simple education-based marketing methods help focus attention on your credibility and ability to effectively communicate, as well as educate. They include the following:

- **Conduct Seminars and Workshops:** Facilitating seminars and workshops reinforces the perception of your expertise while showcasing your ability to teach and communicate. Additionally, the seminar setting provides the appropriate venue for talking to potential clients in a non-threatening, non-selling setting.
- **Present at Professional Conferences:** Members of your target audience often meet at conferences to exchange ideas and keep abreast of developments. Delivering presentations in this type of venue allows you to get face-to-face with potential clients in a far more personalized way than does direct mail. Additionally, it provides the opportunity to demonstrate your ability to effectively communicate and teach and to showcase your expertise. While you may not get paid for these speaking engagements, the contacts and referrals are of far more value than an honorarium would be. "The key is taking technical material and making it fun for the listener."[28]
- **Publish a Newsletter:** Even a single-page newsletter sent once every month or quarter provides the dual benefits of enhancing your credibility — if competently done — as well as providing repeated visibility to your targeted audience. Be sure to include your contact information for requests for further information.
- **Publish Articles:** Publishing is the coin of the realm for most academics and experts. By publishing articles — especially those that are peer-reviewed — your credibility, reputation, and name recognition are enhanced. Beyond scholarly journals, look to publish articles in the trade or professional publications of your target audience. A good place to start in finding the best publication to reach your audience is the *Encyclopedia of Associations*. Articles of specific interest can be subsequently forwarded as part of a direct-mailing campaign to your targeted audience.
- **Participate in Newspaper, Television, and Radio Interviews:** Dr. Phil may have been an expert for a long time, but he wasn't a widely recognized expert until he appeared on *The Oprah Show*. Appearing on or being quoted in any venue of this nature strongly reinforces your recognition as an expert.

[27] *The Testifying Expert*, (February 1996), 4.
[28] Public speaking helps experts market their business, *The Testifying Expert*, (January 1995), 5.

Conducting an expert witnessing practice as a business is a significant endeavor that requires education and attention. Of course, these are two of the attributes that allowed you to become an expert in your field. Ask your trusted advisors — your lawyer, your accountant, and other experts that you may know — what they would advise for the best way to execute your business plan. And remember, as in any business, marketing is both essential and difficult. "It is really hard to market yourself if you're the product."[29]

[29] *The Testifying Expert*, January 1995, 5.

Appendix

Expert Witness Resources

There are several resources available to expert witnesses, including online directories, newsletters, and listservs, which can enhance the expert's business and help locate potential referral sources. Below is a sampling of those resources.

Directories

An internet search for expert directories will yield scores of sites. Some will allow you to list for free; others charge a fee. Most will list biographical information, your area of expertise, and how you can be contacted. Some online directories include:

www.ewitness.com: This site has a free directory list of experts and consultants in a variety of fields. It specifically mentions that their experts are "available for case review and trial testimony."

www.expert4law: This site contains a basic listing of experts in different fields.

www.expertwitness.com: This site "has been providing forensic scientist, medical experts, and various consultants to the legal and business community since 1996." Searches on this site are free.

www.witness.net: This is the site for the Expert Witness Network, which is targeted to the professional. The Network "helps you reach legal professionals across the country who are searching for your expertise and services to assist in preparing their case."

www.expertnetwork.com: This site allows clients to contact listed experts directly, but charge a finder's fee if the client decides to hire the expert.

www.expert-registry.com: This site claims to serve as a "who's who" of experts.

www.lexpertsearch.com: This site is designed to assist attorneys in locating "university professors" as well as professionals.

www.megalaw.com/expert: This site lists a number of additional links to expert directories and other resources for experts.

Newsletters

The Testifying Expert, published by LRP Publications, is a monthly newsletter that provides up-to-date information on the latest state and federal cases affecting expert witnesses, including rulings on Daubert and Frye motions. The Testifying Expert is highly recommended for any expert witness who expects to testify in court. You can contact LRP Publications at 1-800-341-7874.

Listservs

EXPERT-L is one of many listservs specially designed for expert consultants. Experts can request and get information from each other, find job referrals, and get up-to-date information on litigation issues. This listserv also allows experts to keep up with the latest trends in expert witnessing. You can find out about and subscribe to EXPERT-L by going to http://lists.mega-link.net/archives and follow the appropriate links.

Bibliography

Alexander, R. (2001, April). Jury duty in California: An overview of jury trials. Consumer Law Page [on-line]. Available: www.consumerlawpage.com

Angell, M. (1996). *Science on trial: The clash of medical evidence and the law in the breast implant case.* New York: W.W. Norton & Company.

Anonymous. (2001, April). *Daubert* now becomes the rule in the rules. *Defense Counsel Journal,* 68 (2), 248–250.

Anonymous. (1999, January). Experts on experts. *ABA Journal,* 85, 64–69.

Attorney's comment about fees spurs experts' reaction, advice. (1996, June). *The Testifying Expert,* 4 (6), 3.

Clifford, R. C. (1990). *Qualifying and attacking expert witnesses.* Santa Ana, CA: James Publishing Group.

Binder, R. L. (2002, November 11). Liability for the psychiatrist expert witness. *American Journal of Psychiatry,* 159, 1819–1825.

Branch, T. W. From the "Frye"-ing pan into the tire. Albuquerque, New Mexico: Branch Law Firm.

Brostoff, S. (1999, March 29). Insurers praise U.S. Supreme Court for giving judges power on 'expert' testimony. *National Underwriter,* 103 (13), 2, 22.

Capra, D. J. (2000, December 11). Evidence rules receive changes effective December 1: Part 2. Horsham, PA: LRP Publications, *Federal Discovery News,* 7, (1).

Cheever, J. M. & Naiman, J. (1993, February 22). The view from the jury box. *National Law Journal.*

Coniglio, John P. (2002, January). The expert witness: A primer on your activities. *Professional Safety,* 47 (1), 34–39.

Crane, Mark. (1999, January 11). How do expert witnesses get away with lying? *Medical Economics,* 76 (1), 152–164.

Detlefsen, R. R. (2001, May). Confronting hostile experts in the court of public opinion. *The Metropolitan Corporate Counsel,* 20.

Dombroff, M. A. (1984, August). Prepare and present your expert witness. *For The Defense.*

Driessen, P. K. (2003, March 16). 214-year-old law jeopardizes war against terrorism. *The Tampa Tribune,* p. 6.

Experts get strict on billing procedures. (1994, September). *The Testifying Expert,* 2 (9), 6.

Fayette Circuit Court. Information for jurors: Juror handbook. Available: www.aoc.state.ky.us/fayettecourts.

Feder, H.A., (2000). *Succeeding as an expert witness: Increasing your impact and income.* New York: Van Nostrand Reinhold, p. 39.

Finger, A. L. (1999, March 22). How to be your own best expert witness. *Medical Economics,* 76 (6), 96–100.

Fleming, R. D. (1999, October). Hazards of expert witnesses: Disclosing work product and limiting testimony. *Defense Counsel Journal,* 66 (4), 538–554.

Geraghty, K. The code as expert witness. Available: www.ama-assn.org.

Gray, C. B. (2002, December 11). Damage control. *The Wall Street Journal,* A18.

Harts, D. M. (1999, October). Reel to Real: Should you believe what you see? *Defense Counsel Journal,* 66 (4), 514.

Haydock, R. & Sonsteng, J. (1994). *Advocacy: Examining witnesses: direct, cross and expert witnessing.* Eagan, MN: West Publishing.

How to make your written report work for you. (1996, January). *The Testifying Expert,* 4 (1), 3–4.

Huber, P. W. (1993). *Galileo's revenge: Junk science in the courtroom.* New York: Basic Books.

Hunter, T. A. (1992, November 8-13). Some hazards of being an expert witness. Paper presented at the Winter Annual meeting of the American Society of Mechanical Engineers, New York.

Irrational legal exuberance. (2002, October 15). *The Wall Street Journal,* A20.

Insult and tort injury. (2003, March 14). *The Wall Street Journal,* A10.

Jensen, E. G. (1993). When "hired guns" backfire: the witness immunity doctrine and the negligent expert witness. *University of Missouri at Kansas City Law Review,* 62, 185–210.

Jones, R. T. (1985, Summer). Impeaching your opponent's expert. *The Brief.*

Kesan, J. P. (1996). A critical examination of the Post-*Daubert* scientific evidence landscape. *Georgetown Law Journal,* 85 (5).

Lubet, S. (1998). *Expert testimony: A guide for expert witnesses and the lawyers who examine them.* Boston: National Institute for Trial Advocacy.

Malone, D. M. & Zwier, P. J. (2000). *Effective expert testimony.* Notre Dame, IN: National Institute for Trial Advocacy.

Mandell, M. S. (1999, June). *Kumho*: Some clarity – but not the last word – on experts. *The Testifying Expert,* 7 (6), 3–4.

McCloskey, S. S. (2001, Winter). Recent developments in Civil Procedure and Evidence. *Tort and Law Journal.*

McCurley, M. & Eyck, C. A. (2001, March). *Daubert* and the admissibility of expert testimony in child custody disputes. *The Matrimonial Strategist*, 18 (2), 1.

Moore, M. V., Johnson, G. G., & Beard, D.F. (1999). Liability in litigation support and court testimony: is it time to rethink the risks? *Journal of Legal Economics*, 9, 53–63.

Murphy, J. P. (2000, Fall). Expert witnesses at trial: Where are the ethics? *The Georgetown Journal of Legal Ethics*, 14 (1), 217–239.

Not a parody. (2003, January 10). *The Wall Street Journal*, A10.

Nunnally, K. D. (1987). Use of experts. State Bar of Texas Professional Development Advanced Personal Injury Law Course, 2.

Pierson, E. (1998). *1999 Witley expert witness update: New developments in personal injury litigation.* New York: Aspen Law and Business.

Rabinoff, M. A. & Holmes, S. P. (1996). *The forensic expert's guide to litigation: The anatomy of a lawsuit.* Horsham, PA: LRP Publications.

Reilly, R. F. (2000, October). Accountants' considerations of *Daubert*-related decisions on valuation expert testimony. *The National Public Accountant*, 45 (8), 12–14.

Reynolds III, E. (1987). The selection and use of the defense expert. State Bar of Texas Professional Development Program, Experts in litigation: a performance enhancement course.

Rice, J. A. Twelve angry men? Think again. Available: www.jri-inc.com.

Roisman, A. Z. (1998, March). Attorney assesses what *G.E. v. Joiner* means for testifying experts. *The Testifying Expert*, 6 (3), 3–4.

Rossi, F. F. (1911). *Expert witnesses.* Chicago: American Bar Association.

Sacks, M. E., Esq. (1995). *An overview of the law: A guide for testifying and consulting experts.* Horsham, PA: LRP Publications.

Savage, D. G. (1999, May). Putting the brakes on junk analysis. *ABA Journal*, 85, 38–39.

Scott, D. M. (1999, May/June). Scientific v. nonscientific expert testimony: The admissibility distinction that never was. *Commercial Law Bulletin*, 14 (3), 22–23.

Index

E

F

P

Q

R

S

T

U

V

For Product Safety Concerns and Information please contact our EU
representative GPSR@taylorandfrancis.com
Taylor & Francis Verlag GmbH, Kaufingerstraße 24, 80331 München, Germany

www.ingramcontent.com/pod-product-compliance
Lightning Source LLC
LaVergne TN
LVHW021111300926
849160LV00009B/687

* 9 7 8 0 3 6 7 2 2 9 3 3 7 *